Between
Apartheid and
Capitalism

Between Apartheid and Capitalism: Conversations with South African Socialists / Alex Callinicos, ed.
First published January 1992
Bookmarks, 265 Seven Sisters Road, London N4 2DE
Bookmarks, PO Box 16085, Chicago, Il. 60616, US
Bookmarks, GPO Box 1473N, Melbourne 3001, Australia
Copyright © Alex Callinicos and Bookmarks
ISBN 0 906224 68 3

Printed by Cox and Wyman Limited, Reading, England

Bookmarks is linked to an international grouping of socialist organisations:
AUSTRALIA: *International Socialists*,
GPO Box 1473N, Melbourne 3001
BELGIUM: *Socialisme International*,
Rue Lovinfosse 60, 4030 Grevignee
BRITAIN: *Socialist Workers Party*,
PO Box 82, London E3 3LH
CANADA: *International Socialists*,
PO Box 339, Station E, Toronto, Ontario, M6H 4E3
DENMARK: *Internationale Socialister*,
Ryesgade 8, 3, 8000 Arhus C
FRANCE: *Socialisme International*,
BP 189, 75926 Paris Cedex 19
GERMANY: *Sozialistishe Arbeitersgruppe*,
Wolfsgangstrasse 81, W-6000 Frankfurt 1
GREECE: *Organosi Sosialistiki Epanastasi*,
PO Box 8161, 10010 Omonia, Athens
HOLLAND: *Groep Internationale Socialisten*,
PO Box 9720, 3506 GR Utrecht
IRELAND: *Socialist Workers Movement*,
PO Box 1648, Dublin 8
NORWAY: *International Socialister*,
Postboks 5370, Majorstua 0304 Oslo 3
POLAND: *Solidarnosc Socjalistyczna*,
PO Box 12, 01-900 Warszawa 118
SOUTH AFRICA: *International Socialists of South Africa*,
PO Box 18530, Hillbrow 2038
UNITED STATES: *International Socialist Organisation*,
PO Box 16085, Chicago, Il. 60616

Between Apartheid and Capitalism: Conversations with South African Socialists

Edited by Alex Callinicos

Bookmarks
London, Chicago and Melbourne

Abbreviations

ANC	African National Congress
AWB	Afrikaner Weerstandsbewiging
AZAPO	Azanian People's Organisation
BC	Black Consciousness
CAL	Cape Action League
CAST	Civic Associations of the Southern Transvaal
CCAWUSA	Commercial, Catering and Allied Workers Union of South Africa
COSATU	Congress of South African Trade Unions
DP	Democratic Party
DTA	Democratic Turnhalle Alliance
ET Group	Economic Trends Research Group
FAWU	Food and Allied Workers Union
FOSATU	Federation of South African Trade Unions
FT	**Financial Times**
IDASA	Institute for a Democratic Alternative for South Africa
IFP	Inkatha Freedom Party
ISSA	International Socialists of South Africa
KP	Konserwatiwe Party (Conservative Party)
LRAA (or LRA)	Labour Relations Amendment Act 1988
MK	Umkhonto weSizwe
MWT	Marxist Workers Tendency of the ANC
NACTU	National Council of Trade Unions
NMC	National Manpower Commission
NUM	National Union of Mineworkers
NUMSA	National Union of Metalworkers of South Africa
PAC	Pan Africanist Congress
PWV	Pretoria/Witwatersrand/Vereeniging
SACCAWU	South African Commercial, Catering and Allied Workers Union
SACCOLA	South African Consultative Committee on Labour Affairs
SACP	South African Communist Party
SADF	South African Defence Force
SALB	**South African Labour Bulletin**
SAP	South African Police
SSC	State Security Council
SWAPO	South West African People's Organisation
UDF	United Democratic Front
UWUSA	United Workers Union of South Africa
WM	**Weekly Mail**
WOSA	Workers Organisation for Socialist Action
ZANU-PF	Zimbabwe African National Union-Patriotic Front

Contents

Foreword / 7

Editor's Introduction / 11

1. Mark Swilling:
   The Dynamics of Reform / 41

2. Devan Pillay and Karl von Holdt:
   Strategy and Tactics / 55

3. Jeremy Cronin:
   The Communist Party and the Left / 76

4. Colin Bundy:
   Reform in Historical Perspective / 91

5. Moses Mayekiso:
   Socialists and the Trade Unions / 105

6. Neville Alexander:
   National Liberation and Socialist Revolution / 114

Afterword: Social Contract or Socialism?
   The Agenda of the South African Left / 137

Notes / 155

Index / 165

Alex Callinicos is a leading member of the Socialist Workers Party in Britain. He teaches Politics at the University of York and is the author of numerous books, including: **The Revolutionary Ideas of Karl Marx, The Changing Working Class** *(with Chris Harman),* **South Africa between Reform and Revolution, Trotskyism, Against Postmodernism** *and* **The Revenge of History.**

Foreword

The body of this book is made up of a series of interviews I conducted with some leading South African socialists in the wake of the unbanning of the African National Congress and the release of Nelson Mandela in February 1990. All but the last, with Neville Alexander, took place in November or December 1990. My aim was to explore with them the future for socialism in South Africa in the light of both the prospect of a negotiated transfer of political power to the black majority in that country and the apparent collapse of any alternative to capitalism as a result of the 1989 revolutions in Eastern Europe. These are matters on which, as should become plain, I have very definite opinions of my own. My hope was that the interviews would be genuine conversations involving an interplay of views, and thus help to clarify the options available to the left in South Africa. I leave it to the reader to decide how well this collection fulfils my intentions.

I am grateful, in the first place, to Neville Alexander, Colin Bundy, Jeremy Cronin, Moses Mayekiso, Devan Pillay, Mark Swilling and Karl von Holdt, for agreeing to be interviewed and for allowing me to publish the results. Others, notably David Kaplan, Jon Lewis and Eddie Webster, provided very helpful background interviews. I would also like to thank Professor Hermann Giliomee for his hospitality and for helping to clarify my understanding of National Party strategy. Without the help of the Nuffield Foundation, which provided me with a Small Grant, the Department of Politics at the University of York and a private benefactor I would have been unable to visit South Africa and conduct the associated research. I am also indebted to the Marxist Theory Group at the University of the Western Cape, who organised the conference where I first delivered the afterword as a paper. None of the above can, of course, be held to account for the editorial material in this book: the general introduction, chapter introductions, notes and afterword are all my own work and my own responsibility.

I would like, finally, to thank the comrades of the International Socialists of South Africa and the Workers Organisation for Socialist Action. Without their kindness it would have been hard to produce this collection; without their existence there would have seemed little point.

Note on terminology

Some reference to the racial distinctions created by white domination in South Africa is unavoidable. I follow the convention of referring to the entire oppressed population as black; apartheid involved then differentiating between Africans, Coloureds and Indians. May this terminology soon become obsolete.

Note on the interviews

The interviews are printed in chronological order. Questions are printed in italics, except in Chapter 2, where the participants in the three-cornered conversation are indicated by their initials.

Introduction

On 2 February 1990 FW de Klerk, the State President of South Africa, announced in his speech at the state opening of parliament, that he was unbanning the African National Congress, the South African Communist Party, and the Pan Africanist Congress. Nine days later Nelson Mandela, the symbol of black resistance to white minority rule, was released from Victor Verster prison. These moves marked the open commitment by the ruling National Party to seek a negotiated settlement of South Africa's crisis with the mass movement against apartheid headed by Mandela and the ANC. The euphoria which greeted de Klerk's speech and Mandela's release was immense, not simply in South Africa but among all those throughout the world who had supported the struggle against apartheid.

It soon became clear that, in Mandela's own words, there would still be no easy walk to freedom. The violence which erupted on the Witwatersrand in July and August 1990 between supporters of the ANC and of Mangosuthu Buthelezi's Inkatha Freedom Party highlighted the struggle being waged by the de Klerk regime to determine the nature and outcome of the negotiating process. Interwoven with these conflicts was another debate taking place chiefly among the opponents of apartheid, particularly in the powerful workers' movement, about the kind of economic and social order which would replace white domination. The interviews which form the body of this book are concerned with the connection between these two processes—the political transition to a non-racial democracy in South Africa and the struggles to shape the 'post-apartheid' economy. The purpose of this introduction is to outline the historical context in which they are unfolding.

De Klerk's Strategy

The speed of political change in 1990 took commentators of all views by surprise.[1] The National Party (NP), the architects of a system of racial domination and segregation unparalleled in its scale, the suffering it caused, and the brutality with which it was defended, now committed themselves to its dismantling. They also undertook the unthinkable—the pursuit of a negotiated settlement with the main resistance movement, the ANC, whose political survival would not permit it to settle for less than a non-racial democracy based on universal suffrage in a unitary South Africa. An apparently irreversible movement away from apartheid had begun. 'If you think we are going to cancel this, forget it,' said the Minister of Finance, Barend du Plessis. 'We've jumped.'[2]

Why did de Klerk and the NP jump? The answer lies in the profound crisis which South African society has experienced since the mid 1970s. Apartheid first evolved at the end of the nineteenth century, was further elaborated after the formation of the Union of South Africa in 1910 and was then developed into an enormously complex, ideologically rationalised system once the NP had captured power in 1948. It amounted to a highly repressive set of controls on the black majority underpinned by white political domination. These controls went far beyond the denial of citizenship rights to blacks; through the pass laws in particular they provided for the state regulation and direction of Africans' movement around the country.[3] The effect was to provide the white-controlled mines, farms, and factories with a vast supply of cheap black labour. Apartheid thereby promoted the rapid development of industrial capitalism in South Africa for almost a century, from the discovery of gold on the Witwatersrand in 1886 to the boom of the 1960s and early 1970s.[4]

Over the past 20 years, however, it has become increasingly clear that apartheid is a fetter on the further development of capitalism. Economic growth gave way to chronic stagnation. Real gross domestic product grew at an annual rate of 4.9 percent between 1946 and 1974, peaking at 7.8 percent a year in 1971-4; the growth rate then slumped to 1.9 percent in the subsequent decade to 1984, and 1.5 percent in the 1980s as a whole.[5] Interacting with this economic crisis has been the development of popular insurgency on a quite unprecedented scale, starting with the Soweto rising of June 1976 and culminating in the nation-wide wave of township insurrections of 1984-6. While the level of township resistance has fluctuated enormously, one other trend had been far more consistent—the emergence of a black workers' movement organised largely in non-racial unions independent of the state. In the shape of the Congress of South African Trade Unions (COSATU), the mainstream of this movement has increasingly identified politically with the ANC.

Underlying the growth of black resistance and trade union organisation has been a profound structural change. The emergence, as a result of nearly 30 years of economic growth after the Second World War, of a relatively developed industrial economy in South Africa, in which manufacturing now contributed a larger proportion of output than mining and agriculture combined, led to a shift in the balance of power between white capital and black labour. The relative scarcity of white workers, to whom apartheid had guaranteed a monopoly of skilled jobs, forced employers to break the colour bar and increasingly to recruit Africans for semi-skilled and even skilled positions. The long term effects of this process became clear in the 1970s and 1980s. The proportion of Africans in non-manual and skilled manual jobs more than doubled as a proportion of total employment, from 6.0 percent in 1965 to 14.1 percent in 1985. The same study found that, between 1976 and 1985, explicitly racial discrimination had become less important and 'differential grade attainment'—the fact that Africans were still largely concentrated in less-skilled grades—more important in explaining the gap between white and African wages. Moreover, there was a tendency for racial discrimination to decrease the more skilled the job concerned. 'Signs of an emerging integration of the labour market are clear,' the author of the study concluded. Blacks' share of personal income rose from less than 30 percent in 1960 to 41 percent in 1985.[6] Racial inequalities remained enormous, and the suffering especially of rural Africans was greatly intensified by drought and recession in the 1980s, but blacks' movement into semi-skilled and skilled jobs gave them power and confidence they never had before.

After PW Botha became leader of the National Party in September 1978, the regime responded to these socio-economic and political changes with a series of limited concessions, notably the legalisation of African trade unions in 1979 and the introduction in 1983 of a new constitution which allowed the two minority black communities recognised by apartheid law, the Coloureds and Indians, to elect their own chambers of parliament. This amounted to what Hermann Giliomee and Lawrence Schlemmer call 'reform-apartheid', summed up in the words of 'a prominent business leader: "We Afrikaners ... must try to find the secret of sharing power without losing control." '[7] In other words, Botha's aim was to preserve a modernised version of white domination, in particular by widening the regime's base to include a layer of privileged black intermediaries. The strategy was a disastrous failure: it simply whetted the black appetite for more radical change and alienated a large section of the NP's traditional base among the poorer white farmers and the Afrikaner petty bourgeoisie and working class. In 1984-6 Botha found himself caught between two fires. On the one hand there was black insurrection in the townships, increasingly identified with the exiled ANC. On the other there was white reaction orchestrated by the Conservative Party (KP), which broke away from the NP in 1982, and fascist organisations like the Afrikaner Weerstandsbewiging (AWB). Botha's eventual response was to impose, on 12 June 1986, a nation-wide state of emergency which unleashed the most concerted wave of repression in South African history. Reforms did not completely halt under the Emergency—in 1986 the pass laws were abolished. But such concessions seemed to be part of a highly controlled process of change directed by the 'securocrats' in the South African Defence Force (SADF)-dominated State Security Council (SSC) and National Management System (NMS) where the making and implementation of policy were increasingly concentrated under Botha.

A main factor indeed in the power-struggle between Botha and de Klerk which ended with the former's resignation on 14 August 1989 was the growing antagonism felt by the National Party cabinet and parliamentary caucus towards the SSC/NMS hierarchy which seemed to be supplanting them. De Klerk's accession to the state presidency after the parliamentary election of 6 September 1989 marked the triumph of the party over the securocrats.[8] But de Klerk then went much further than any previous Nationalist politician. He first allowed the ANC-aligned Mass Democratic Movement to hold a series of large demonstrations and then freed all those still serving jail sentences imposed in the 1964 Rivonia treason trial except for Mandela himself. Finally he made the leap of February 1990.

Behind these moves lay a recognition that Botha's reform strategy had failed and that the Emergency had only temporarily contained the pressures for more radical change. The prospect of chronic economic stagnation confronted the regime. A massive flight of capital at the height of the political crisis in September 1985 had forced Pretoria to impose a partial moratorium on the foreign debt South Africa had rapidly built up at the beginning of the decade. South Africa therefore had to make very heavy repayments on a foreign debt totalling $21.2 billion at the end of 1988, but was unable to raise fresh capital abroad, for political rather than economic reasons. South Africa was 'underborrowed' by the standards of an economy of its size and sophistication, but Western bankers were afraid of risking capital on so politically unstable a country. The debt burden imposed a straightjacket on South Africa, limiting economic growth. As the **Financial Times** put it:

> The main constraints on growth remain government inability to curb spending ... and the need to run a sizeable current account surplus to repay foreign debt. In practice, this places a 3 per cent ceiling on economic growth. Recent experience has shown that any faster growth sucks in imports at an unsustainable rate, and puts unbearable pressure on the gold and currency reserves...
> The irony is that by forcing South Africa, a developing country, 'to export capital like a little Switzerland'... Africa's most dynamic economy is having to be reined in before it can achieve the sort of 5 to 7 per cent growth of which it is theoretically capable, and which is necessary if black unemployment and a near 3 per cent [annual] population growth rate is to be absorbed.[9]

The implications of slow growth for South Africa's long term stability were grim. One NP economist, Jan Lombard, calculated that only eight million of the 12 million-strong workforce were in formal employment. Projections envisage the number of unemployed rising to six or even eight million people by the end of the century. Barend du Plessis, the Finance Minister, warned: 'Unless we can get growth going now, by the mid 1990s it will be virtually impossible for *any* government to govern this country, because of the number of unemployed.'[10]

A political settlement was a precondition of economic recovery. Only such a settlement bore any hope of ending the economic sanctions imposed by most Western governments in response to the 1984-6 crisis and, more important, attracting foreign capital back to the country. And no negotiated solution could succeed unless it included the ANC. It had emerged from the risings of the mid 1980s politically hegemonic among the black population. The repression during the Emergency had seriously weakened popular organisation in the townships; it had not, however, significantly reduced support for the ANC. Moreover, the one form of mass organisation which continued to grow under the Emergency—the union movement—had become increasingly openly aligned with the ANC and its allies in the SACP. Even the most sympathetic of Western governments, Margaret Thatcher's, pressed the regime to talk to its chief opponent.

Formidable though these pressures on de Klerk were, he had certain important cards in his hands. Long-term economic trends might be working against the regime, but the political balance of forces was much more favourable. Above all, the state's military powers remained vastly greater than those of its opponents. Neither the risings of the mid 1980s nor the military campaign of the ANC's armed wing, Umkhonto weSizwe (MK), had succeeded in significantly undermining Pretoria's effective monopoly of organised violence. Alfred Nzo, then Secretary-General of the ANC, confessed in January 1990: 'We must admit that we do not have the capacity within our country to intensify the armed struggle in any meaningful way.'[11] Moreover, de Klerk could bargain from a position of relative strength within the white camp itself. The NP preserved its unity during the Botha succession crisis in the first half of 1989 and swallowed de Klerk's February 1990 initiative with little visible dissent. Electorally, too, the challenge of the far right seemed to have been contained: the KP's 31 percent share of the white vote in the 1989 election was only marginally higher than the total extreme right vote in the previous election of May 1987. The NP vote dropped to 48 percent, but de Klerk could in pursuit of his new course also count on the support of the liberal Democratic Party (DP) which received 20 percent of the white vote.

As Ronald Aronson put it, 'de Klerk's brilliant manoeuvre was to release Mandela, unban the ANC, begin the negotiations, and move to end apartheid *before* he was forced to.'[12] In other words, by seizing the initiative and effectively conceding the resistance's more important demands, de Klerk put himself in a position to control the transition to a non-racial democracy, and thereby to ensure that the outcome preserved the domination of the existing white capitalist class. Compare, for example, the East German regime in October and November 1989. Erich Honecker and then Egon Krenz lagged behind events: every concession they made, had it been offered months, weeks or even days earlier, might have stabilised the situation. But because the reforms were wrenched out of a regime reluctantly adapting itself to a popular movement it could no longer hope to crush, they merely fed the demand for a complete overturning of the East German state. By contrast, by keeping ahead of events, de Klerk could hope to keep control of them.

What, then, was de Klerk's goal? He broke with NP tradition on one decisive issue. Rather than, as Botha had, tinker around with apartheid, he conceded the main demand of the resistance, for a constitution based on one person, one vote, instead of on the kind of ethnically based 'federal' system which government reformers had previously envisaged. The main pieces of apartheid legislation—the Group Areas Act, the Population Registration Act, the Land Acts of 1913 and 1936—were repealed in 1991. The tribal Homelands or Bantustans which had been the regime's excuse for denying black citizenship rights during the apogee of apartheid in the 1960s and 1970s were plainly doomed.

Nevertheless, the constitutional settlement pursued by the regime would be based on universal suffrage but would be designed to prevent the black majority exercising effective control over the country's destiny. In August 1991 the NP unveiled proposals for 'Constitutional Rule in a Participatory Democracy' which so hedged universal suffrage with restrictions as almost to nullify it. In the first place, they envisaged a two-chamber parliament. The First House would be directly elected by one person, one vote. Its decisions, however, could be vetoed by an Upper, or Second House, made up of an equal number of representatives from each of nine proposed regions. Every party winning a minimum number of votes in a region (perhaps as low as ten percent) would qualify for an equal share of the seats from that region. As Patrick Laurence commented, 'the plan clearly provides for overrepresentation of minority parties in the second house ... to cite a hypothetical example, the Conservative Party with ten percent of the vote in the thinly populated Northern Cape will earn as many seats as the African National Congress with sixty percent of the vote in the densely populated PWV [Pretoria/Witwatersrand/Vereeniging] region.'[13]

Secondly, there would be a collective presidency, consisting of the leaders of the three to five parties with the largest number of seats in the First House. The presidency, whose chair would rotate on an annual basis, would appoint an all-party cabinet to implement its decisions. Thirdly, considerable powers would be vested in the governments of the nine regions, whose executive committees would again involve power-sharing by the three to five largest parties in the popularly elected legislative councils. Finally, a third tier of government would be in the hands of non-racial unitary local authorities replacing the crazy quilt-work of white and black municipalities. These authorities would also be elected by one person, one vote—though, in an extraordinary provision presumably intended to dilute the influence of the squatters thronging into South Africa's cities, owners and renters of property would receive an extra vote.

This last proposal, along with other details, was probably less the regime's bottom line than part of an opening bid in the substantive negotiations on the constitution which the NP hoped to hold with the ANC. Nevertheless, it was clear enough that through constitutional provisions such as those outlined in these proposals de Klerk intended, without explicitly appealing to racial or ethnic concepts such as 'group rights', to give the white minority a veto over significant changes and to institutionalise 'power-sharing' at all levels of government. In other words, the NP was seeking, not to abandon power, but to remain in government as the permanent coalition partners of the ANC, no doubt at least initially retaining in its hands such key portfolios as Defence and Law and Order. But to realise this objective de Klerk needed not merely a favourable constitution but also a significant bloc of seats in a majority-rule parliament.

And so the regime set out to make the NP a rallying point for conservative black forces. Hence the NP's decision to open its ranks to all races—a move which, amazingly given the party's history, actually evoked some response. A number of MPs belonging to the Labour Party, the main 'Coloured' organisation to have participated in the Tricameral Parliament, have joined the NP.

These plans went considerably further, as Patti Waldmeir of the **Financial Times** reported:

> Government officials now speak openly of forming a 'Christian democrat' coalition, or alliance, to claim the middle ground of South African politics, and to oppose a 'socialist' coalition led by the ANC and its close ally, the South African Communist Party ... They believe that most whites, a potentially large number of the 3m coloured ... and 1m Indians, and a significant number of black Africans would support such a grouping. The Zulu Inkatha Freedom Party—which claims 2.2 million members and shares many policies with the reborn Nationalists—would be a likely member; they argue a surprisingly large number of moderate blacks might vote for Mr FW de Klerk...
>
> 'I have no doubt that when the real electoral process is in [the] offing ... there will be a moderate alliance in which the National Party will play an important part which has more than an even chance to win an election,' Mr de Klerk told the **Financial Times**.[14]

This strategy had direct implications for the regime's attitude towards the ANC. Ronnie Bethlehem, economic consultant to Johannesburg Consolidated Investments, made an interesting analysis of the divisions within the NP. He distinguished between, on the one hand, the 'pragmatists', who were committed to a negotiated settlement, and, on the other, the 'strategists and racial ideologues', for whom the ANC 'remains an enemy to be destroyed. What differentiates [the latter] ... is only a matter of degree. Strategists will use the negotiation process to first weaken before crushing the other' while '[i]deologists remain committed to crushing directly through a deliberate use of force.' Bethlehem warned that the strategists and ideologists might drag

> De Klerk further in the direction of believing, or hoping, that out of a discrediting of the ANC ... he will be able to achieve a coalition of anti-ANC support that would give him victory in an eventual open election.
>
> That would be a dangerous delusion. Whatever its shortcomings, the ANC remains the only organisation that could possibly deliver the support of a large majority of blacks on a negotiated settlement on a new constitution, just as it is only the NP that could do the same with the whites...

... De Klerk and the whites need to come to terms with ... the ... reality... that they need the ANC and need it badly. One could almost say that if the ANC did not exist it would be necessary to invent it ... Control over the black dimensions of SA society has been lost by government and the business community, and both need a credible partner with whom they will be able to work to bring about the political transformation that has become an essential precondition for a liberation of the economy.[15]

But even if de Klerk did believe that he needed the ANC as the only political force which could persuade militant workers and youth to accept a negotiated settlement, he might still agree with the 'strategists' that it was necessary to keep the ANC under pressure. That way, he could force it onto the defensive, making its leaders more likely to concede a settlement favourable to the NP, and create a climate in the townships which would help the 'Christian Democratic Alliance' to win votes when elections came in 1993 or 1994. At any rate, the most plausible interpretation of the regime's behaviour in the eighteen months after the great breakthrough of February 1990 was that some such consensus prevailed in government circles. Initially the two sides seemed to be moving quite rapidly towards substantive negotiations.

In particular, the Pretoria Minute, agreed on 6 August 1990, appeared to go quite a long way towards meeting the ANC's terms for creating 'the necessary climate for negotiations' set out in the Harare Declaration adopted by the Organisation for African Unity a year before. The Harare Declaration demanded the unconditional release of all political prisoners, an end to bans and restrictions on organisations and people, the removal of troops from the townships, an end to the state of emergency, the repeal of all repressive legislation and an end to political executions. In exchange for government promises to expedite an amnesty for political prisoners and 'give immediate consideration' to repealing the most obnoxious security legislation, 'the ANC announced that it was now suspending all armed action with immediate effect'.[16]

The regime, however, continued to drag its feet; it took another year for terms to be agreed which would allow political exiles to return to South Africa. Far more seriously, fighting burst out in the townships of Johannesburg.

Inkatha and the state

The violence between the supporters of Inkatha and of the ANC on the Witwatersrand claimed 1,500 lives between its outbreak in July 1990 and April of the following year. It seemed to confirm one of the main themes of NP propaganda, that South Africa was a society of minorities, in which conflict between tribally based black groups was as significant as that between black and white. A 'senior Nationalist' told the **Financial Times**: 'The violence made the point that apartheid failed to make: that the problem of ethnicity, black ethnicity, is real in South Africa.'[17] Any attempt, however, to present the ANC-Inkatha struggle as essentially tribally based and operating independently of the regime, is profoundly misleading. Such an analysis in the first place leaves out of account the role of the South African state in encouraging, and indeed sometimes inventing tribal differences, especially after Hendrik Verwoerd, architect of 'grand apartheid' formulated the policy of 'separate development' in the 1950s.[18] Moreover, as John Carlin of the London **Independent** observed:

> To refute the 'tribalism' argument is so simple that it is almost embarrassing. The violence in the townships around Johannesburg had been an extension of the violence in Natal province, where some 4,000 people have died in the past five years. Those killing each other in Natal are all Zulus—Zulus who support the African National Congress and Zulus who support Inkatha...
>
> In Soweto, to name but one of the battlegrounds of recent weeks, Zulu residents make up approximately 40 percent of the population. They have been on the receiving end of the Inkatha hostel dwellers knives just as much as the Xhosas, Sothos, Shangaans and all the rest. Zulus have been patrolling the streets of Soweto at night to defend their homes against attack by Inkatha warriors.[19]

The struggle between the ANC and Inkatha was a political struggle—between non-racial revolutionary nationalism and conservative tribal nationalism—not a battle between tribes. Seeing the conflict in political terms does not, however, explain why Inkatha, more and more clearly established as time went on as the main (though not the sole) aggressor in the violence, was able to win mass support, and in particular to organise armed phalanxes of migrant workers from the all-male hostels dotting

South Africa's cities in rampages through ANC areas. Greg Ruiters and Rupert Taylor argued after the first wave of violence on the Rand:

> What is distinctive about the pattern of conflict between mainly Zulu-speaking hostel dwellers and mainly Xhosa-speaking squatter camp inhabitants is not the ethnic lines of division but that the participants and victims of the violence are those who have been among the most severely exploited and disadvantaged by the apartheid system.
>
> Whilst hostels—the epicentres of the violence—house the most degraded section of the working class, the squatter camps are home to a predominantly jobless under-class caught up in a culture of poverty. Both environments are characterised by a lack of any personal privacy or recreational facilities, and by severe overcrowding. Hostel dwellers have around three square metres of their own living space. On average the number of people living in one shack is six.
>
> Under the migrant labour system, Zulu-speaking workers, living in cold, dark, single-sex hostels are separated from family life and forced to perform the worst kind of dirty work in foundries, other heavy industry and municipalities. Their escape is to return to the increasing impoverishment of the rural areas which they call home.
>
> The position of squatters is worse: living in a state of constant poverty and insecurity, without basic services and sanitation, these people lack fundamental human rights...
>
> In order to explain the extent of the violence attention must be given to underlying tensions within community politics and the union movement. In particular, both hostel dwellers and squatters have not been integrated into formal organisational structures. Both groups were perceived as outsiders, politically marginal to local struggles...
>
> To township people, hostel dwellers are regared as 'mogus' or 'amagoduka' (fools or wanderers). Zoned in buildings often situated on the edges of established communities, they do not have strong social networks which link them to townships. The fact that many hostels, such as those in Soweto, are situated near railway stations means hostel dwellers rarely need to enter townships...
>
> Zulu-speaking migrant workers in Natal and on the East Rand proved easy to organise and were the backbone of the early unions in the 1970s. In recent years, however,

migrants have found themselves displaced in industrial union structures by younger and more politicised shop stewards.

Central to this has been the rise of COSATU and its challenge to FOSATU's syndicalist policies of co-existence of all workers. FOSATU tended to emphasise workers' factory unity rather than political unity. Since COSATU's emergence, hostels have no longer been central to union organisation as was the case earlier, and migrants who are unionised have experienced a degree of alienation.

Union strategies have failed to adequately address hostel dwellers' grievances and the increasing insecurity of the lowest paid workers who are largely disqualified from reform initiatives relating to housing, pensions and medical aid schemes. Unions have not effectively blocked retrenchment which affected the unskilled disproportionately, and COSATU recently undersigned a proposed Labour Relations Act which compromises domestic and farm workers.[20]

It is easy to see how, in these circumstances, Zulu-speaking migrant workers, alienated from the unions and the ANC-aligned civic organisations, should have been relatively responsive to Inkatha's organising drive in the hostels, especially since it had the tacit backing of the employers and the police. The image, cultivated by Inkatha, of the old Zulu kingdom could act, in the words of Marx's famous analysis of religion, as 'the heart of a heartless world', giving meaning to lives characterised by the most appalling poverty and oppression.[21] And in Inkatha's paramilitary formations, brandishing guns and 'cultural weapons', the powerless could develop a sense of power, as they spread terror through the townships. The cycle of violence unleashed by the fighting which began in July 1990 could also feed on the conditions endemic in the vast squatter settlements which had grown up around the cities as influx control collapsed in the mid-1980s. Struggles over access to resources between township and squatter-camp dwellers, over control of the camps themselves by groups seeking to extract protection money, and over the taxi routes which represented the easiest means for Africans to accumulate capital, often received political expression. Sometimes the different sides supported the same organisation, usually the ANC. Sometimes their conflicts became aligned with the national struggle between the ANC and Inkatha.[22]

The violence in the townships was thus to some extent an explosion of accumulated tension created by the poverty and oppression inflicted on the black majority under apartheid. Nonetheless it also reflected the strategy being pursued by some of the main political actors in the national drama. Was it merely an accident that the ANC-Inkatha conflict spread from Natal to the Witwatersrand—politically and economically the heart of the country—within months of the unbanning of the main anti-apartheid organisations?

The prospect of substantive negotiations between the ANC and the regime presented Buthelezi with the danger of being marginalised. The violence—among whose immediate causes was an Inkatha recruiting drive on the Rand—showed that Inkatha was not merely a regional force in Natal, but a national force. In the following months, Buthelezi could once again bask in the warmth of international attention. Moreover, Mandela, previously blocked by the rest of the ANC leadership from meeting Buthelezi, had two highly publicised attempts at reconciliation with him.

And then there was the question of the state. Evidence rapidly accumulated of police complicity in Inkatha's violent rampages. Initially it seemed plausible to interpret this as evidence of disaffection within the SAP, many of whom were supporters of the KP, AWB and other far-right formations. But it soon became clear that support for Inkatha came from the very top of the regime. In July 1991 the Johannesburg **Weekly Mail** and the London **Guardian** published Security Branch documents which revealed that at least R250,000 had been paid by the SAP to fund Inkatha activities such as a rally in Durban on 25 March 1990; the rally was followed by some of the worst fighting in the townships of Pietermaritzburg, the heart of the ANC-Inkatha struggle in Natal. Major Louis Botha of the Durban SB explained in a memorandum before the rally,

> During our discussions it became clear that the actions and political manoeuvres of the ANC were a matter of concern to the chief minister [Buthelezi], especially if one considers the shrinking Inkatha membership figures ... [h]e is very suspicious of overtures from the ANC which according to him would make it easy for the ANC hierarchy to destroy him if he joined the ANC...[23]

'Inkathagate' caused a political sensation, since it confirmed beyond any doubt that the government was not a neutral bystander in the ANC-Inkatha conflict. It came, however, after other revelations which suggested that state subsidies for Inkatha were part of a much more extensive strategy directed against the ANC. Thus Nico Basson, an ex-major in military intelligence, gave the **Independent** details of 'Operation Agree', an SADF plan approved at the end of 1988 by the Minister of Defence, Magnus Malan, and the Minister of Foreign Affairs, Pik Botha. Designed to prevent SWAPO from winning the 1989 independence election in Namibia, this campaign of dirty tricks was a 'trial run' for a similar operation in South Africa itself. 'The SADF is buying AK-47 weapons on a large scale notably from Mozambique and supplying these to Inkatha,' Basson alleged. 'The violence in the townships... had been deliberately orchestrated by the SADF,' the **Independent** reported. ' "They could stop it immediately if they wished," Mr Basson said'.[24] Other evidence uncovered the role of the SADF in importing pro-Inkatha gangs from Natal and members of its own special forces, notably the Fifth Reconnaissance Regiment, to carry out some of the most 'professional' massacres, for example, that in which 13 mourners were shot dead at a funeral vigil in Alexandra on 27 March 1991.[25]

Inkathagate released a flood of yet more revelations. Inkatha's union front, UWUSA, turned out, according to an SAP document, to be 'a project under the control of the South African Police'.[26] De Klerk himself confirmed that an elite unit of 150 Inkatha fighters had been trained at an SADF base in the Caprivi Strip in Namibia before the territory became independent in 1990.[27] Captain Dirk Coetzee, ex-head of the SADF's death squad, the Civil Co-operation Bureau, suggested from exile that black mercenaries who had served in Koevoet, the brutal police counter-insurgency unit in Namibia, and in the South African-backed guerilla movement Renamo in Mozambique were being used against the ANC in the townships. Behind these various forces, he suggested,

> is a loose alliance between the dirty tricks departments of the military and the police, involving personnel and equipment from South Africa's frontline wars, notably in Rhodesia, Mozambique and Namibia... the strategy, based on that used by the security forces against SWAPO, is one

of undermining the African National Congress and boosting its political opponents in order to cheat it at least of overall political control of the country.[28]

De Klerk sought quickly to limit the damage caused by Inkathagate, demoting Malan and the Minister of Law and Order, Adriaan Vlok. He denied all knowledge of the payments to Inkatha. If true, this suggested that the securocrats were well entrenched in power despite Botha's fall. Far more likely, de Klerk had at least tacitly acquiesced in a strategy whose effect would be to weaken the ANC and therefore to make it a less formidable rival at the negotiating table and at the ballot box.

Negotiation and mass struggle: the ANC response

Inkathagate offered a welcome opportunity for the ANC to regain the initiative. Until then, the widespread impression had been created, among supporters as well as opponents of the ANC, that it had allowed itself to be outmanoeuvred by de Klerk. 'Too clever for Mr Mandela' was how the **Independent** summed up the State President during his triumphal tour of Europe in April 1991. Its correspondent, John Carlin, argued:

> No one has been more naive than Mr Mandela, who from the day he left prison and virtually every time he opened his mouth during the next six months, described Mr de Klerk as a 'man of integrity'. Mr Mandela, and other 'moderates' in the ANC leadership took Mr de Klerk at face value. They believed that the government and the ANC would be equal partners in the voyage to the 'New South Africa', that apartheid would go and they, as the natural majority party, would glide into power...
> In one sense Mr Mandela's trust was not misplaced. Mr de Klerk *will* remove apartheid from the statute books. He *will*, when it suits him, release the political prisoners. But this was never the issue; he knew from the day he came to power that this was what had to be done. The real issue was to retain power, to perpetuate white privilege and the economic status quo after apartheid had gone.[29]

Recognition of the extent to which the ANC had floundered in response to de Klerk's subtle and ruthless strategy was widespread within the movement itself. ANC-SACP leader

Ronnie Kasrils, then still on the run from the police because of his role in MK, wrote in an article co-authored by Mandla Khuzwayo and published at the beginning of 1991:

A number of worrying signs seem to indicate that we are losing the initiative:
*The ANC was unable to protect township residents against the terror;
*The ANC has been unable to hold the regime to the terms of the agreements it has signed. The regime seems to be able to decide for itself when and how it will implement the Pretoria minute;
*de Klerk has scored a number of international break-throughs and the overseas anti-apartheid movement is being marginalised in its respective countries;
*the National Party is increasingly managing to set its timetable as the timetable for negotiations. The regime talks about the process lasting until the next white election;
*our branches and mass organisations are relatively weak and have little effect on the direction of the negotiation process.[30]

The toll taken by the Inkatha violence on the mass base of the 'Revolutionary Alliance' of the ANC, SACP and COSATU was undeniable. One 'senior ANC official' told the **Financial Times**: 'people are beginning to say, if we join the ANC we will be killed'. Such fears help to explain the fact that by mid 1991 the ANC, despite polls consistently showing that it had the support of a majority of Africans, had little more than 250,000 members, compared to Inkatha's claimed membership of 2.2 million.[31] COSATU national organiser Jeremy Baskin wrote:

The violence seriously affected the unions, whose activists were often in the forefront, digging trenches and organising community self-defence. Workers absented themselves from work to help defend their families. Few wanted to attend union or COSATU local meetings. Unions such as NUMSA [National Union of Metalworkers of South Africa], with large membership in township hostels, were hardest hit. At least five NUMSA-organised factories saw clashes between Inkatha and non-Inkatha forces, and a planned strike at USCO steel was abandonded after 19 NUMSA members were killed in an attack on the Sebokeng Hostel.[32]

The most common explanation within the Alliance for these setbacks was that, as Kasrils and Khuzwayo put it, 'the prevalent orientation to the negotiations process ... has not fully explored the development of all-round mass struggle'. The solution, according to ANC-SACP 'hard-liners' such as Kasrils and MK chief of staff Chris Hani, was not to abandon negotiations but rather to regain 'the strategic initiative' by ensuring that 'the ANC—and mass struggle under the leadership of the ANC— determines the pace and process of negotiations'. Thus Kasrils and Khuzwayo called for 'a combination of mass action and negotiations', the implication being that 'mass action' had been neglected by the ANC leadership since February 1990.[33] The difference between ANC 'moderates' and 'hard-liners' were thus essentially ones of emphasis, over the relative weight to be given to mass struggle and negotiations in the transition to a non-racial democracy in South Africa.

What Kasrils and Khuzwayo call 'the prevalent orientation in the negotiations process' has in fact much deeper roots in the politics of the ANC and the SACP. These old allies had long been committed to a two-stage strategy of revolution, in which national liberation, ridding South Africa of apartheid, must precede the struggle for socialism. **The Path to Power**, the new programme adopted by the SACP at its 7th Congress in 1989, reaffirmed the analysis underpinning this strategy, namely that apartheid is a 'Colonialism of a Special Type', in which 'the colonial ruling class with its white support base on the one hand and the oppressed colonial majority on the other are located within a single country'. The removal of this 'internal colonialism' requires 'a national democratic revolution which will overthrow the colonial state and establish a united, democratic and non-racial South Africa. The main content of this revolution is the national liberation of the African people in particular, and the black people in general.'[34]

But how was the 'national democratic revolution' to be achieved? Guerilla warfare, the classic method used in Third World revolution, proved, by common acknowledgement, to be a dead-end, despite the heroism of the MK fighters and the political importance of their armed action during the 1980s in building up popular support for the ANC in the townships. The fundamental reason for the failure of MK lay in the non-existence in South Africa of the social base of successful guerilla wars elsewhere, a substantial small-holding peasantry. The African population of South Africa is overwhelmingly proletarianised—perhaps 80 percent are wage-labourers and their dependants. At least two thirds of all Africans live either in the cities or in areas (for example, resettlement camps integrated into the main conurbations) that are 'functionally' urban.[35] **The Path to Power** acknowledged that *'ours cannot be a classic guerilla-type war primarily based on the winning, over time, of more and more liberated territories, nor are there immediate prospects of inflicting an all-round military defeat on the enemy.'*[36]

What, then, was the alternative to a classical guerilla-type war? The 1984-6 risings led many ANC activists to envisage the overthrow of the regime by some kind of mass insurrection: analogies were sometimes drawn with the Iranian Revolution of 1978-9. And in its propaganda at the height of the risings, the ANC leadership behaved as if it believed that such an insurrection was on the agenda. It called on the masses to render South Africa 'ungovernable' and to arm themselves with weapons seized from police stations and barracks.[37] It is not clear, however, that even then the ANC leadership seriously expected the regime to be brought down by popular risings. Its revolutionary rhetoric was accompanied by a series of meetings with white establishment figures, of which the most important was that in September 1985 between delegations headed by ANC President Oliver Tambo and Gavin Relly, Chairman of the Anglo-American Corporation. The most plausible interpretation of the ANC leadership's real strategy was that it had a long-term orientation towards a negotiated settlement. Various methods—armed struggle, mass strikes, township risings, peaceful protests, and economic sanctions—were all intended both to force the regime to talk to the ANC and ensure that the terms of any deal were as favourable as possible to the resistance.

Certainly, once the State of Emergency had put an end to the risings, the ANC leadership proceeded rapidly to draw up its negotiating agenda, most notably in a set of 'Constitutional Guidelines' issued in October 1988 which spelt out in somewhat more detail the liberal democracy envisaged in the 1955 Freedom Charter, which remains the ANC's main programmatic document. Careful efforts were made to cultivate what the SACP General Secretary, Joe Slovo, called the 'forces for change', 'including recent defectors from the white laager' who could be won to 'the broadest possible front of struggle against the racist autocracy' under the leadership of 'the revolutionary forces' proper headed by the ANC.[38] Candidates for such a role included white liberal groups such as the Five Freedoms Forum and the Institute for a Democratic Alternative for South Africa, as well as sections of the Democratic Party. Meanwhile, Mandela emerged as the key link between the government and the ANC, meeting first Botha and then de Klerk and receiving a string of guests in prison. Indeed, commencing with the illness in late 1988 which led to his removal from Pollsmoor prison in Cape Town to Victor Verster prison in Paarl, Mandela opened what amounted to preliminary negotiations with the regime. In particular, a letter to Botha in a correspondence intended to define the conditions for formal talks was adopted by the ANC as the basis of the Harare Declaration.[39]

The ANC-SACP leadership sought to assuage its activists' fear of a sell-out as part of the same process. **The Path to Power** insisted: 'Armed struggle cannot be counterposed with dialogue, negotiation and justifiable compromises, as if they were mutually exclusive categories.'[40] The tenor of ANC strategy was indicated by the title of one of the preparatory documents for the Congress-dominated Conference for a Democratic Future held in December 1989: 'Negotiations as a Terrain and Method of Struggle'.[41] This reorientation reflected outside pressures as well as the evolution of the situation inside the country. A meeting of the ANC National Executive Committee with representatives of COSATU and the Congress-aligned United Democratic Front in Lusaka on 6-7 June 1989 concluded: 'Negotiations are again a matter of discussion because of the manoeuvres of the imperialists which have some support from our long-established friends.'[42] Among these 'friends' now supporting a negotiated settlement were the black-ruled frontline states of southern Africa, which had suffered terribly from Pretoria's policy of regional destabilisation, and the USSR, now eager to liquidate all its regional conflicts with the United States. The superpower-sponsored New York accords of 22 December 1988, under which South African and Cuban troops were withdrawn from Angola and independence granted to Namibia, offered a precedent for a peaceful solution in South Africa itself.

An increasingly explicit commitment to a negotiated settlement had thus become the cornerstone of the Congress

Alliance's strategy well before February 1990.[43] But what has become clear since February is the extent to which this commitment has been greatly reinforced by what amounts almost to a parallel negotiating process under way between the leaders of the most powerful component of the 'Revolutionary Alliance', the organised working class, and representatives of big capital. The emergence of a black workers' movement centred on COSATU, which at its Fourth Congress in July 1991 claimed 1,258,853 members, is the single most important achievement of the anti-apartheid struggle over the past two decades.[44] COSATU-affiliated unions were able to grow in size and organisational strength despite the State of Emergency. In alliance with the National Council of Trade Unions (NACTU), which is led by supporters of the PAC and the Black Consciousness movement, they mounted a campaign of resistance, notably a three-day stayaway on 6-8 July 1988, which eventually forced the state and the employers to agree to repeal the anti-union Labour Relations Amendment Act (LRAA).

From COSATU's inception in December 1985, its office bearers such as General Secretary Jay Naidoo had been open in their political support for the ANC. The federation's first three years, however, were marked by a bitter internal dispute between 'workerists' and 'populists'. The former were identified with the most important union grouping to have preceded COSATU, the Federation of South African Trade Unions (FOSATU).[45] They comprised worker activists and the mainly white intellectuals who had both pioneered the development of an indigenous South African Marxism in the 1970s and 1980s and helped to found the independent unions after the Durban strikes of 1973. The workerists rejected the ANC-SACP two-stages strategy, arguing that the objective of working-class struggle should be socialist revolution; at the same time, however, they placed primary emphasis on building strong, politically independent trade union organisation, tending to reject, at least as an immediate priority, the need to lay the basis of a workers' party as a socialist alternative to Congress. The populists, by contrast, contended that the proper place of the workers' movement was as part of a broad alliance led by the ANC and concentrating on the 'national-democratic struggle against apartheid.'[46]

The conflict between workerists and populists was intense

during the early part of the Emergency, perhaps reaching its climax at COSATU's Second Congress in July 1987 and the attendant split in the Commercial and Catering Workers Union of South Africa (CCAWUSA), one of the most militant unions in the country.[47] Even at this stage, however, the workerist-led unions, such as the National Union of Metalworkers of South Africa and the CCAWUSA majority, were outnumbered by the populists, headed by the National Union of Mineworkers. COSATU followed most of its affiliates, including NUMSA, in adopting the Freedom Charter at its 1987 Congress, thus symbolically identifying itself with the ANC. By the Third Congress in July 1989 a substantial degree of political convergence between populists and workerists had been established, largely on the former's terms. The Congress endorsed conditions for talks with the government only marginally different from those of the Harare Declaration. The extent of the workerists' retreat was indicated by an interview before the Congress with Moses Mayekiso, General Secretary of NUMSA and the best known independent socialist in the workers' movement. Endorsing 'broad alliances with people who are anti-apartheid', he declared that 'the solutions to our country's problems will finally come through negotiations. I don't believe that we will be able to get to Pretoria and oust Botha from those buildings.'[48]

The process of incorporation of COSATU into the Congress Alliance accelerated after the unbanning of the ANC and the SACP. A tripartite 'Revolutionary Alliance' of the three organisations was formally established on 9 May 1990.[49] Perhaps of more significance (especially since the ANC seems largely to have ignored its commitment to consult its Alliance partners) was the rapid emergence of the SACP as a force within COSATU. The party's launch as a legal organisation on 29 July 1990 was marked by the announcement of an Interim Leadership Group including four prominent trade unionists—Moses Mayekiso and John Gomomo of NUMSA, and Chris Dlamini and Sydney Mafumadi, respectively First Vice-President and Assistant General Secretary of COSATU. Dlamini and Mafumadi turned out subsequently have been quite long standing SACP members, but Mayekiso's and Gomomo's adhesion seemed to symbolise the way in which a generation of working class leaders associated with the FOSATU tradition were now rallying to the party. Karl von Holdt, editor of the **South African Labour Bulletin**, pointed to the irony that while 'the SA Communist Party was launched as a legal party amidst mass support from workers and youth' and 'speaks with confidence of its future role', 'in the rest of the world, Communist Parties are falling from power, falling apart, changing their names'.[50]

The contemporary role of the SACP is explored in the interviews below, notably those with two of its leaders, Jeremy Cronin and Moses Mayekiso. Undoubtedly, one factor in the Party's ability to attract trade unionists previously highly suspicious of its record was Joe Slovo's celebrated pamphlet **Has Socialism Failed?**, first circulated in January 1990. In it Slovo acknowledged that the East European revolutions of 1989 had been 'popular revolts against unpopular regimes', and, abruptly dumping a 60 years' tradition in which the party in South Africa had loyally toed the Moscow line, demonstrated the systematic discrepancy between Marx's and Lenin's theory and Stalinist practice.[51] Although denounced by die-hard Stalinists like the Robben Island veteran and Pietermaritzburg leader Harry Gwala, the pamphlet allowed Slovo and his co-thinkers to relaunch the SACP as the 'Party of Democratic Socialism'.[52] This image, of a party in the process of democratically remaking itself, must help to explain why former workerists such as Mayekiso came to believe that they could transform the SACP into the kind of workers' party some at least had aspired to build in the early 1980s.

The SACP's evolution, however, soon provided a reminder that 'democratic socialism' is often a way of referring to social democracy. Slovo went out of his way after February 1990 to reassure big business that the 'Revolutionary Alliance' had no intention of expropriating them. Thus the **Financial Times** reported:

> Building socialism ... is not the immediate goal of the ANC, Mr Slovo says. 'The economy of South Africa the day after the ANC flag flies over the Union Buildings in Pretoria will be exactly the same as the day before,' he asserts. 'You can't transform it by edict without risking economic collapse.'[53]

Slovo's arguments were symptomatic of the general direction in which thinking was moving inside COSATU itself. Increasingly this focused on two ideas. The first is that the labour movement should be seeking to secure an 'accumulation strategy' which would enhance the international competitiveness of South African manufacturing industry and improve the welfare of the masses. The second idea is that achieving this objective would in all likelihood require a 'social contract' between COSATU, an ANC government and big business. These ideas are discussed at length below, notably in the interview with Karl von Holdt and Devan Pillay and in my afterword. It cannot, however, be stressed sufficiently that attempts theoretically to justify such an approach—notably by the Economic Trends (ET) Research Group associated with COSATU, and by von Holdt, who has emerged as the most sophisticated South African defender of a left reformist strategy—represent in part a rationalisation of what is increasingly becoming the union movement's practice.[54]

Two examples may help illustrate the point. First COSATU's and NACTU's ultimately successful campaign against the LRAA necessarily involved the unions in negotiations with the government and the employers' South African Consultative Committee on Labour Affair (SACCOLA). The outcome was the 'Laboria Minute', agreed by the four parties on 13 September 1990. This includes important gains for the workers' movement, notably government promises to repeal the most obnoxious provisions of the LRAA and to extend union rights to agricultural and domestic workers. But the minute also provided for the unions participating in the state's National Manpower Commission (NMC).[55] It soon became clear that restructuring the NMC was an important component of a strategy by the COSATU leadership to institutionalise bargaining between unions, employers and the state. Thus Geoff Schreiner, COSATU's chief negotiator with SACCOLA and the regime, argued the unions' aim 'must be to develop a structure which we can use to help build the power of the working class to achieve our medium and longer-term objectives.' He strove to show that such a strategy would not compromise the union movement's ability to wage mass struggle, though in doing so he revealed how far the COSATU leadership was prepared to go to restrain such struggles under a social contract:

> COSATU should never allow itself to accept limitations on the right to mass action *as a precondition* for participating in the institution [ie. the NMC]. This is quite different from the case where, *as part of* a social contract negotiated

through the institution, the trade union movement could conceivably agree to restrict strikes (on certain issues, for a certain period of time) provided the trade-offs were sufficiently attractive.[56]

An example of what such a policy might mean in practice was provided by the bitter occupation or 'sleep in' at the Mercedes Benz plant in East London between August and October 1990. The dispute pitted a majority of the workforce against, not merely management, but the leadership of NUMSA and the two full-time senior shop stewards at the plant, since the workers rejected the employers' pay offer accepted by the union in the National Bargaining Forum for the auto industry. The dispute was complex, reflecting a history of internecine disputes within the East London car unions. The Mercedes workers were accused of sectionalism—or, as Karl von Holdt called it, 'factory tribalism', since NUMSA was strongly committed to centralised bargaining in the face of efforts by big employers to use plant negotiations as a means of exploiting weak organisation in some factories. Yet the occupation seems to have been an assertion of a tradition of highly politicised militancy in the plant. Christoph Köpke, chairman of Mercedes Benz South Africa, told von Holdt: 'we have had a factory with worker control since 1987. Supervisors used to clock in and then lock themselves into their offices for the whole day. They didn't dare go out on the assembly lines.' Some workers would wear mock AK-47s or bazookas strapped to their backs on the assembly lines. Mercedes workers devoted unpaid overtime to build a special car for Nelson Mandela. Köpke complained: 'that car came off the line with nine faults. In this company cars don't come off the line with less than 68 faults. In Germany, about 13 faults. Normally it takes 14 days to build that [type of] car—Mandela's car was built in four days!' [57]

It required the direct intervention of 'Revolutionary Alliance' heavyweights—Moses Mayekiso of NUMSA, Steve Tshwete of the ANC and Joe Slovo of the SACP all addressed a mass meeting on 20 September—to end the Mercedes occupation. The danger was that, in order to preserve centralised bargaining, the union leadership would snuff out the strong workplace organisation that had developed in factories like Mercedes. Moreover, restraint of shop floor militancy could actually breed the 'factory tribalism' denounced by defenders of NUMSA official policy. The heyday of the social contract under the 1974-9 Labour government in Britain saw workers react to national pay restraint by seeking sectional solutions. This was the case with the British Leyland toolmakers when they fought in 1977 to preserve pay differentials and the miners when their leaders imposed on them that same year the incentive scheme which played such a decisive role in creating the divisions in the coalfields during the Great Strike of 1984-5.[58]

The Mercedes dispute, with its polarisation between, on the one hand, shopfloor workers, and, on the other, full time officials and shop stewards highlighted the tendency towards the emergence of a trade union bureaucracy within COSATU. Jeremy Baskin, in his generally sympathetic history of the federation, acknowledged the increasing concentration of power in the hands of the full-time officials:

> A central tenet within COSATU and its affiliates is that workers control the organisation and officials are simply full-time functionaries ... In practice, however, worker leaders have found great difficulty combining a full day's work with the demanding tasks of union leadership. Some have managed to negotiate time-off from their workplaces, while others have the status of full-time shop stewards, essentially free to come and go as they please ... Major union issues cannot be adequately tackled and grasped on a part-time basis. As a result, it is usually union officials who wield real power, with elected worker leaders and executive committees acting as a check on the abuse of that power. The [full-time] union general secretary is more likely to be better known, and called upon to resolve a crisis within the union than the [lay] president. Since the principle of worker leadership was originally intended to ensure hands-on leadership by workers, the system clearly no longer works effectively. While the principle is retained, officials wield more power than ever before, and effective worker leaders no longer spend much time at work.[59]

The South African workers' movement has developed a healthy tradition of democratic debate and rank and file control. Nevertheless, the growing bureaucratisation of the movement has led to some ugly episodes, perhaps most notably that which led to the expulsion of several officials and members of the Cape Town branch of the Food and Allied Workers Union (FAWU) in May 1990. Political issues were involved: the union leadership was closely associated with the SACP while the expellees were accused of being supporters of the Marxist Workers Tendency of the African National Congress, the sister organisation of the British Militant. Nevertheless former FAWU General Secretary Jan Theron argued that underlying the dispute was 'organisational corruption'. He noted various trends in FAWU and other unions. Thus, 'the centralisation of power [in union head offices] and the scale of unions nowadays tends to separate leadership from membership ... there is also a different kind of worker leadership emerging. There are increasingly in leadership people who are higher paid, and whose experience of unionism and workers control and democracy, does not go back very far.' Moreover, 'in many cases full time shop stewards are functioning as officials ... Yet they are not subject to the controls to which officials are subject, because they are regarded as workers in terms of the constitution.'[60] Such trends could only be reinforced by the institutionalised involvement of COSATU in 'tripartism' with the employers and the state.

Apologists for COSATU strategy argue that it will help create the conditions for a transition to socialism. Thus John Saul claimed that it represents a process of 'structural reform' whose most important characteristic is that it will 'leave a residue of further empowerment—in terms of growing/enlightenment/class consciouness, in terms of organisational capacity—for the vast mass of the population, who thus strengthen themselves for further struggles, further victories.'[61] More cautiously, Alec Erwin, NUMSA Education Officer and perhaps the key intellectual in the ex-workerist group which rallied to the Congress Alliance in the late 1980s, suggested that the ET Group's proposals for a quasi-Keynesian strategy of 'growth through redistribution' 'will be a transition to socialism if the working class can achieve this by its own organisational strengths.'[62]

Yet the evidence—in South Africa itself and in countries such as Britain and Italy which experienced versions of a social contract in the second half of the 1970s—is that attempts to reform capitalism through a process of institutionalised bargaining are actually disempowering. They encourage the concentration of power at the very top of the workers' movement and, through the restraint they impose on shopfloor militancy, undermine workplace trade union organisation. Certainly, whatever the protestations of Alliance leaders, negotiations have acted since February 1990, not 'as a terrain and method of struggle', but as an alternative to struggle, to the detriment of the mass movement. 1990 saw a major strike wave, with a record four million working days 'lost', many of them in the public sector where union organisation had hitherto been weak. Though focused on wage-demands, the strike wave, which actually began in late 1989 with major and violent disturbances on the railways and at South African Breweries, was undoubtedly stimulated by the propects of political change opened up in February.[63] The response of the ANC and its allies was, however, to restrain this militancy. Thus Mandela twice intervened personally to persuade workers to call off strikes—first, of Soweto teachers in March 1990 and then at Soweto's Baragwanath hospital that May.

The reign of terror launched by Inkatha on the Reef in July 1990 proved to be a turning point. At the end of that month NUMSA began balloting its members in the metal industry over whether they should strike in support of the demand for a R2 hourly increase agreed by the union's national bargaining conference the previous February. Despite the violence in the townships, 53 percent of NUMSA members took part, voting by an overwhelming majority—63,000 to 6,000—for strike action. The union leadership decided, however, to call the strike off, on the grounds that 'a major industry strike could have sparked off further widespread violence in the Pretoria/Witwatersrand/ Vereeniging (PWV) area' where NUMSA's membership is concentrated.[64] This decision represented the loss of a major opportunity to overcome the division inside the working class which Inkatha and the state were exploiting by seeking to involve hostel-dwellers (many of whom are metalworkers) in a struggle to remedy their material grievances. The abandonment of the metalworkers' strike, while typical of NUMSA leadership's policy of threatening national strikes and then calling them off at the last moment, helped to transfer the initiative from the mass movement to its opponents.

Even Inkathagate did not lead to a break in this pattern. Instead the ANC signed a peace accord with the government and Inkatha on 14 September 1991. The ceremony was preceded by another terrible outburst of violence on the Rand in which 110 people died in five days, many of them in incidents bearing all the hallmarks of attacks by state undercover forces. True to form,

Buthelezi denounced the accord even before it had been concluded, while armed Inkatha supporters demonstrated outside the Johannesburg hotel where it was signed. Not surprisingly, a stayaway hastily called by the ANC for 16 and 17 September was an ignominious flop. The weeks following the signature of the accord saw no significant abatement in the township slaughter. They were, however, marked by a veering leftwards on the part of COSATU. The federation first withdrew from the NMC in protest against the government's failure adequately to implement the Laboria Minute and its imposition of Value Added Tax, and then, with NACTU, called a general strike against VAT on 3-4 November. The strike's size—between three and four million workers took part—was a tribute to the basic class organisation created in the previous two decades. But the COSATU leaders' demand that the government set up a 'macro-economic negotiating forum' to allow bargaining between unions, employers, political parties and the state indicated that it saw the general strike as a means of forcing the ruling class into a social contract. The overriding priority was the pursuit of class compromise. Despite the ritual invocation by COSATU and SACP leaders in particular of the need to combine negotiations and mass struggle, the 18 months after February 1990 thus saw negotiations act as a fetter on mass struggle.

Conclusion

Despite the problems and setbacks experienced by the mass movement in South Africa, there are many reasons for optimism. The very strategy pursued by the ruling class since February 1990—of incorporating the ANC through a negotiated settlement and COSATU through a social contract—is an indication of the fact that this movement, and in particular the organised working class are too powerful to be crushed by repression. The November 1991 VAT strike, the biggest in South African history, showed the limits of Inkatha's reign of terror. Anyone with direct experience of the trade unions, and of the civic associations and youth congresses in the townships, is struck by the vitality of the South African working class. Moreover, the 'Revolutionary Alliance' is very far from being a monolithic entity. The ANC's first national conferences after its return from exile, in December 1990 and July 1991, revealed an assertive rank and file unwilling passively to accept the dictates even of Mandela, who cultivated a regal style after his release from prison, let alone of an executive committee too long accustomed to top-down leadership. COSATU's democratic traditions have not yet been snuffed out by the tendencies to bureaucratisation discussed above. Even the SACP is experiencing *glasnost*, thanks both to Slovo's denunciation of the past and the influx of ex-workerists. Indeed, the abortive Moscow coup of August 1991 exacerbated an identity crisis arising from the difficulty of defining a distinctive role for the SACP within the Alliance.[65] As the interviews both with Mark Swilling and Moses Mayekiso indicate, many ANC activists seek to promote the development of an autonomous 'civil society' capable of waging struggles whatever the nature of the government that emerges from the negotiating process. And the combined impact of South Africa's limited liberalisation and the upheavals in the USSR and Eastern Europe created a ferment of discussion within the mass movement. The transformation of the **South African Labour Bulletin** from, in the late 1980s, an uncritical supporter of the populist wing of COSATU to, after February 1990, a major forum of debate was one of these signs.

Nevertheless, the prospect of a negotiated transition to a non-racial democracy, in a political climate where socialism, the goal of most anti-apartheid activists, has apparently been eclipsed, raises a host of questions. What is the nature of the transition? Can it successfully be accomplished? What place does township violence occupy in this process? Is the best option for the working class movement in South African conditions to pursue a reformed capitalism? Can the SACP be transformed into an authentic socialist workers' party or is it necessary, as groups standing in the Trotskyist tradition—most notably the International Socialists of South Africa and the Workers Organisation for Socialist Action—argue, to build an alternative organisation outside the Congress Alliance? What is the relationship between race, nationality and class? What is the meaning of socialism at the turn of the twentieth century? Many of these questions are addressed in this introduction, the interviews that follow and my afterword. Whatever the reader may think of the views expressed by the South Africa socialists to whom I spoke, and by me as editor and interviewer, the discussions they represent are part of a broader debate essential to the future of the South African left.

Chapter 1
The Dynamics of Reform:
Mark Swilling

Mark Swilling is a researcher and activist with long associations with township civic organisations. He has lectured in the Department of Politics and is a member of the Centre for Policy Studies at the University of the Witwatersrand. Currently he works at the Johannesburg-based urban reform organisation Planact.

If you go back to Verwoerd, his power base was within the state, in the Native Affairs Department. Vorster's powerbase was within the state, in the police. PW Botha's power base was within the state, within the military.* FW de Klerk had no power base within the state. His only power base was within the National Party, and even then he came in on a highly divided vote. His principal objective was to unify the party around a new project. It couldn't be the old project of PW Botha because that was highly discredited: it left power in the hands of the securocrats, which the National Party disliked intensely.†

The mandate that the National Party gave FW was that the NP must retain power, must regain its position in the state as

---

*HF Verwoerd, generally regarded as the architect of apartheid, was Prime Minister from 1958-1966. BJ Vorster was Prime Minister 1966-1978. PW Botha was Prime Minister from 1978 to 1984, when the office was merged with that of State President. Botha resigned in August 1989, to be succeeded after the parliamentary election of 6 September 1989 by FW de Klerk.

†'Securocrats' is the name given to the decision-making apparatus which developed under Botha centred on the State Security Council and the National Management System and dominated by army officers. The militarisation of the executive, which reached its high point during the state of emergency imposed on 12 June 1986, tended to marginalise the National Party parliamentary caucus and even the cabinet.

the governor. Now he couldn't do that around a securocratic policy, because that would have left power in the hands of the securocrats. He couldn't go for a far-right old-style National Party policy, because that would have meant going back in with the Conservative Party, and the economic and political consequences of that would have alienated the econocrats within the state and business. He's very close to business, closer to business than any other National Party leader.

So de Klerk's only real strategic option, as the forces around him started to solidify and pressurise in all sorts of complex ways, was to make this move. Now it wasn't just a voluntarist decision. I've identified five structural factors which made the moment, rather than the man making the moment. There were the changes in the world balance of power and conflict resolution in south western Africa—Angola and Namibia; economic crisis which the econocrats were saying was irresoluble without a political solution; the continuation of resistance and the failure of the Emergency; conflicts within the state between the securocrats and the National Party and unreliability of the security forces because of the Rockman affair* on the one hand and the right wing on the other; and the liberalisation of business. Business from about 1988 onwards were putting the political problem of apartheid on the agenda. Slowly and gradually South African business began to perceive its own interests through the ideological mists as the consequences of delaying the inevitable changes moved from the opportunities list to the threats list.

De Klerk's adminstration has gone through two phases—the 1989 phase and the post-February 1990 phase. In the pre-February phase, the National Party was playing around with a kind of neo-consociationalism—group rights, concurrent majorities, what I call the skin game. Post-February they started to play with the numbers game. They've replaced group rights with majority rights. They've accepted 'the majority should rule', and went for proportional representation as a mechanism for cosociational division. They began to realise that there's one advantage about democracy, and that is that it's a package deal

---

*Lieutenant Gary Rockman, a 'Coloured' member of the South African Police, emerged to prominence after he denounced the SAP massace of at least 23 people in the Western Cape on election day, 6 September 1989. He went on to organise a trade union for police and prison officers.

that includes an electoral system, and electoral systems, as all good gerrymanderers will tell you, can be manipulated in all sorts of very different ways. So you could structure the interests of the minority, who happen to be white, into the political process via the electoral system, rather than via the constitution.

That new dawn was critically important for de Klerk because here he had a way of doing what PW was never able to do. This is to speak a language that the world understands and the ANC understands, and sell something which was palatable, while simultaneously building in a political process that wouldn't fundamentally threaten the white minority, on condition the white minority agreed to be deracialised by accepting a black middle class and the deracialisation of economic power. So the trade-off is essentially white power for minority power.

The real question is whether the whole thing is viable. Now the big buzz word in South Africa today—and I'm partly responsible for introducing the literature—is 'transition to democracy'. In southern Europe, Latin America, and eastern Europe you had what they call non-revolutionary regime transitions, so that you can make the jump from—as Lenin put it—barbarism, but, unlike Lenin, you can do it without a revolution. I think that has provided an extremely useful conceptual and strategic framework for people thinking through how you can manage a transition without detonating the collapse of capitalism. What the National Party have realised is that it's much better to support fully the transition, in fact escalate the pace of transition, on condition you remain in control of the terms of the transition. If you can do this, what may change are the faces and the colours of the people in political power, but the class interests will not be fundamentally changed. So that's what remains in control of the terms, interests rather than individuals.

What's interesting about the Latin American example applied to here is that the Latin American military kept control of the terms of the transition in the interests of a reformed capitalism. And that model applied here means that old white power-holders manage the terms of the transition for the same objective. Coupled to that is what I call the changes industry—the van Zyl Slabberts, the IDASAs, the Five Freedoms Forums etc. There is a phenomenal number of workshops, seminars, discussions, conferences, talks right across the country in boardrooms, in industrial relations seminars, in local-level negotiations, in universities, all over the place.* Basically, it's a winning-hearts-and-minds campaign, to create a multiracial middle class, which would be an absolute precondition for the future state: it cannot survive without that base. So there's a massive amount of American money being pumped into IDASA and other organisations. It's critically important for creating and socialising people with a certain class base.

It's highly politically risky because it's conducted in a language and discourse and a style which workers are not part of. The risk—and this risk is staring everyone in the face now—is that you will create a political democracy of a fairly sophisticated kind, which is workable, but it will be imposed on a highly unequal economic condition, which will in turn trigger a class based politics. The power of the union movement and civic movements in particular is substantial. The chances of the ANC pulling off a demobilising, African-style nationalist project to divert people away from their interests in favour of nation-building are small.

That is why you find all the liberal intellectuals—the Kane Bermans, the Laurie Schlemmers, etc—talking about nation building: they're basically trying to do the ANC's work for the ANC. But the ANC's not talking about nation-building. The ANC hasn't got a hegemonic project at the moment. It's present in the mind of some intellectuals, but a hegemonic project in order to work in the light of the transition has to be different from what it was prior to the beginning of the transition.

Prior to the transition the ANC's project was a multi-class alliance, but the interests that were dominant were those of the popular classes. It's the change industry that's attempting to build the class base for the future ANC. But the ANC's not articulating with it in any very sophisticated way because they constantly find themselves being drawn back into their old base.

This in turn is a major problem for the government. The government wants a strong ANC. Business wants a strong ANC. No one's talking about privatisation any more because they want

---

*Frederik van Zyl Slabbert resigned as leader of the opposition Progressive Federal Party (which later merged to form the Democratic Party) in February 1986 to concentrate on building bridges between white opinion and the extra-parliamentary opposition, founding the Institute for a Democratic Alternative for South Africa.

the ANC to inherit a strong state to control things. Business realises that there are three elites in the game—the ANC elite, the old state elite, and the business elite—and those three can do business with one another. But they need a strong ANC—the ANC's not doing it right. The branches that are being established are becoming very militant because they're drawing on the past and challenging the leadership. So there are some serious problems for the transition-makers. White power's intact, it's unassailable in many ways, and white power can survive, but the National Party can't survive ...

I find the general overview you've given very convincing. But one implication of this whole process is that the National Party, as the central institution integrating ruling-class politics in South Africa, is going to be liquidated. That seems to me the most remarkable thing about the whole process, because it's fairly exceptional for parties of that kind—the obvious analogies with eastern Europe are intriguing here—to participate in their own dismantling.

It's not dismantling, it's transformation. The National Party won't cease to exist. They think they've a good chance of being the future DTA.* They want to be at the centre of a coalition of minorities that will be able, with one-third control of the legislature, to block legislation or alternatively force the ANC into a coalition.

Yes, I understand the strategy, but it nevertheless is quite a major transformation. If you think of comparisons of the National Party with, say, the Christian Democrats in Italy or the Liberal Democratic Party in Japan—parties that are the dominant factor in the state, great apparatuses of patronage and policy co-ordination, etc.—they're not going to play that kind of role any more.

Well, I don't know about that, because one of the non-negotiables may be that the security forces should remain intact under a

---

*The Democratic Turnhalle Alliance (DTA) is a coalition of conservative white and black organisations in Namibia which sought, with Pretoria's backing, to provide an alternative to SWAPO.

National Party minister. It's not like they're disappearing out of the state. The other thing is that they are hoping that their current control of the bureaucracy is going to be a crucial card in the coalition-making, where they will be able to bring into deals agreements concerning whether they will mobilise the bureaucracy in a certain direction or not. They've traded a monopoly on power for a veto of power. I think that's the heart of it.

It seems to me that that's much easier to enforce with respect to the army than it is as far as the state bureaucracy generally is concerned.
You talked about the creation of a multi-racial middle class: well, one crucial factor in the constitution of black middle classes in post-colonial Africa has been their massive occupation of the upper echelons of the state. It's very striking in Zimbabwe—the huge influx of educated blacks, most with a past in the liberation struggle, into the senior civil service. I would have thought it would be hard for the ANC to drop that, particularly if it's going, as you say, to have all sorts of problems about welding together the coalition that it's constructed.

The ANC doesn't want to block it. In fact, there are all sorts of deals going on at the moment to set up training programmes for a future civil service, which will absorb people at a rapid rate mainly into the upper echelons of the state. One effect of Botha's desire to streamline the bureaucracy and cut off some of the fat is that, although it didn't entirely happen that way, at the top levels it did begin to happen.

From the early 1980s a lot of posts were frozen and so you have an ageing top civil service... There's space at the top, which I think is quite important. Also, we are not the same as any other African country. There's a massive absorptive capacity in the parastatals—the Development Bank, CSIR, ESKOM, those kind of large-scale development corporations.* There are already deals being made to absorb people into those positions as preparation for and a training for civil service positions. I'm

*The Development Bank of South Africa, the Council for Scientific and Industrial Research (CSIR) and the Electricity Supply Commission (ESKOM) are all state-owned corporations, or parastatals.

involved in some of that. For example, I'm involved in setting up a school for training civil servants at the Business School.

So preparations are fairly advanced. This is all part of the change industry you were talking about.

No, the change industry are people who massage the soul of the old South Africa to come to terms with the new South Africa. What I've just been talking about is a fairly new development. This is about the nuts and bolts of reconstituting personnel and the power structure. The change industry make people believe that everything's going to be hunky-dory. People who really know what's going on know that's bull.

You said before the interview began that there's a consensus at the top—presumably you mean big business, the National Party and the ANC—about political and economic questions, and that the really controversial issue is that of development. What precisely did you mean by that?

As far as citizenship is concerned, there's agreement that everybody will be enfranchised in a united South Africa, with a bicameral legislature and an executive. The only debate is whether it'll be a strong or a weak executive; that there will be proportional representation; that there will be a decentralised system without federalism. So all that is in broad agreement, for different reasons. The ruling class think that decentralisation is a way of breaking up the majority, whereas the liberation movement thinks that a decentralised system is a good thing for democracy. So what that means is that decentralisation will become contested terrain, which is also good for democracy and pluralism.

On economic issues there's agreement that basically there won't be nationalisation, that we're all involved in the market, that we need to get manufacturing back on track again, that we need to limit financial speculation, that there needs to be some sort of redistribution in order to meet basic needs.

These are macro-economic objectives. Development, by contrast, is micro more than macro. It's about putting projects on the ground. It's about getting resources into processes to deliver goods to make people's lives a bit better. Now my argument is that if you exclude the amount of resources currently spent on health, education, and transport, there is about R5 billion at 1990 prices available within the economy as currently structured, but it is not getting down into the ground. It's not getting down into the ground mainly because of the financial institutions and the way they are structured; the construction industry, which is highly monopolised; the building materials industry, which is cartelised; but also because of the structure of the bureaucracy. We don't have a developmental bureaucracy, we have a colonial bureaucracy for domination.

What this means is that there are basic needs on the ground, there are resources, but we have some fundamental blockages which are rooted in the vested interests that the constitutional transition is not going to dismantle. There cannot therefore be a consensus on development, because it requires tackling those fundamental vested interests. The way in which development is being dealt with by the elites is not to debate it, but try and build a consensus on broad, generalised, opaque objectives rather than on specific mechanisms.

At the level of specific mechanisms, there's a fundamental battle going on, between the unions and civics* on the one hand and the construction industry, Urban Foundation†, financial institutions on the other. But that battle, which links workplace and community-based struggles about the distribution of the social surplus, is not impacting up into the political. The ANC isn't calling for bond boycotts, while at the same time there's a whole bunch of bond boycotts being planned against financial institutions who fund developers who build houses that are cracking up, that are falling apart. If the civics accept the ANC's call, it will have removed a fundamental weapon against the financial institutions.

So when I say the debate is about development what I mean is that, underlying the apparent consensus on politics and on

---

*Civic associations emerged in the townships after the Soweto rising of 1976 to wage struggles around community issues. In the mid-1980s they tended to become politically identified, affiliating to either the ANC-aligned United Democratic Front, or, less frequently, to the Black Consciousness National Forum Committee, and played a crucial part in the township risings of that period.

†The Urban Foundation was set up by liberal big business after the Soweto rising of 1976 to involve the private sector in the townships.

economics, there are battles going on about the reconstruction of society. These are going to blow apart the consensus—not, I think, in a revolutionary, ruptural way, but they're going to play themselves out politically in a pluralistic, democratic framework in all sorts of interesting ways. For example, we're not going to lose our mass-action tradition. The streets are going to become as important as the legislature. The other aspect of this development debate is that the ANC's economic policy document argues for growth through redistribution, whereas business is saying growth with redistribution. My argument is that the fundamental difference between the two positions rests on the ability of civil society to play a developmental role. The ANC's and other documents actually say that if civil society isn't strong and independent and capable of taking on development, the ANC's intended growth-through-redistribution strategy will become a growth-with-redistribution strategy, because there won't be the mobilised capacity from below to take on the financial and bureaucratic system to get the resources down into the ground.

When you talk about civil society you mean primarily the unions and civics?

Well, I would identify those as the two important pillars of civil society. The other important one is the church. And then there's a complex associational life beneath, around and beyond them in civil society, which having a non-welfarist state has made possible, indeed an absolute necessity. One strong tendency within the ANC is to adopt the old socialist rhetoric of 'the state will provide', which is a euphemism for 'the people shall not provide.'

When you talk about rhetoric of a socialist kind, you're thinking of what—the Marxist-Leninist tradition?

Yes. Joe Slovo has made a reasonably impressive attempt to distance the Communist Party from statism, but he hasn't blown all his bridges. To blow all the bridges you have to go back to the Freedom Charter. The Freedom Charter never talks about nationalisation. It talks about transferring wealth to the *people*. Now if you assume the people and the state are the same thing then you can conclude that the Freedom Charter talks about nationalisation. But if you hang on to the distinction between state and civil society, transferring wealth to the people doesn't mean statism. It means going for a potentially new democratic socialism. This is an extension of the concept of governance beyond its traditional meaning—namely, the state has the right of government—to include the right of civil society to govern, and that's inevitably decentralised, localised networks of co-operation, in economic, social and political life, rather than the traditional individualism.

I would say that even within Marxism, although there's the ideology and rhetoric of the collective, in the end the notion 'the state will provide' conceives of the rest of society as individual consumers of services provided by that state. And that is the fundamental error—to look to the state—in Marxism, and I don't see any fundamental break from that. It's beginning to happen in South Africa and other places. But it hasn't been elaborated properly. The instrumentalist view of the state in mainstream Marxism was a fatal error, which has led to very unfortunate results, contrary to the intention.

I'm not sure that it's appropriate to get into a long argument about the history of Marxism, but it does seem to me that the strand you identify, what you call statism—it's also been called socialism from above—is very distinctly present in the socialist tradition, and is best represented by Stalinism and social democracy. But there's also a tradition which stresses the notion of socialism as self-emancipation and which conceives socialism as something which comes from below—perhaps Rosa Luxemburg is the most obvious example...

Paul Hirst recently wrote an article called 'Associational Socialism', and that captures what is seen as very attractive in the civic movements. It retains the associational culture that underlies the civic movements. It also links that associationalism to economic redress.

What implications does all this have for formal political organisation? If you're going to have this diverse set of autonomous organisations in civil society—the unions, the civics, churches, whatever—and you're going to assert interests that

*diverge with the elite consensus that you were describing earlier,
surely that's going to be reflected in the emergence of different
political parties articulating their interests? It sounds to me from
what you're saying that there's no way in which the ANC can
encompass all this.*

No, that is why the ANC is committed to genuine pluralism and
a multi-party system. I think the Communist Party might wake
up from its temporary numbness, especially when the leadership
starts to change. At the regional level the leadership has changed
fundamentally. But outside the Revolutionary Alliance, the PAC
has got a lot of potential for growth. Unfortunately its leadership
is caught in an old classical revolutionary paradigm, which like
many classical revolutionary paradigms doesn't understand
power at all, though they talk about power all the time.

There are a whole bunch of left factions, however, some in
the PAC and the ANC but outside these movements as well, who
have retained their orthodox revolutionary position but are
becoming much more realistic about power. There are the kinds
of people who would be happy to operate in a pluralistic
environment in order to build social movements, without plotting
armed revolution. Those kinds of tendencies will definitely grow.

Because of the overpoliticised nature of South African
society people are going to want a holiday from that, they're going
to want to go to the civic and the union, where you can sit and
talk with whomever, whatever their politics are, about bread and
butter issues, about the defence of living standards. That, I think,
is going to be the major growth area—squatter movements,
housing movements, civic movements, union movements. Social
movements in the true sense of the word, rather than political
parties, are going to be the major growth.

*This error about power—could you define what it is? What's the
mistake the revolutionary left has made about power?*

Revolutionaries have the tendency to set their sights on what is
not possible now and therefore miss out on doing what is possible.
If you gear your whole organisation to the impossible, you are
trying to commit your followers to a faith in something which you
cannot demonstrate is possible now and so you will remain
marginal. People are not going to last the race if you are not

mobilising them around interests which are both immediate and long term. There's not enough energy in ideas, and revolutionaries are obsessed with ideas.

The impossible is a revolutionary seizure of power?

It's impossible in the current context, given the current balance of forces. It's not impossible as an abstraction. The context might change.

It was Trotsky who said that the revolutionary is the most consistent fighter for reforms...

What I say all the time now to reformers is that for reformers to succeed you need revolutionaries who fail. I cause a lot of anxiety among people for saying that. There are two kinds of reformers: there are reformers who believe as a matter of principle and morality that reform is a superior strategy to revolution, and then there are reformers who have come to the conclusion that revolution's not going to work—that doesn't mean we think that reform is a superior strategy to revolution. That's what's happening to a lot of people—they're reformers by default.

And you think there will be a real space in the unions and the civics for the kind of articulation of interests you're talking about to take place?

It's not a prediction, it's a fact. The Orlando East branch of the Soweto civic is controlled by the Africanists. When I give workshops one can't talk about the ANC anymore because when you stand up at the end of the meeting and you sing the national anthem there are PAC signs, Socialist International signs, ANC signs, BC signs—they're all part of the civics. That's a reality which you also find in the unions. Obviously at this stage the ANC, activists who are the most skilled and accessed to resources, are hegemonic. But there is a potential for them to be contested and for an alternative leadership to emerge within the civic. And so you'll have the contestation of civil society taking place, linked to the fortunes of political parties. Political parties will inevitably intervene in civil society to secure their leadership, but what is critical is whether the separation between civil society and political society will remain. If civics are ANC instruments, then there's no hope.

But one could argue on the basis of the experience of the rest of Africa that that is what will happen—there will be a process of nation-building which will swallow up the independent institutions.

Yes, that is what happened in Africa but I don't think it's going to happen here. There are times in history when ideas do override interests, and that is happening here, but it's reinforced by the interests of the civics and the leadership of the civics, who are saying: We're not prepared to become extensions of the ANC. They don't want just to become part of a huge mass movement. And they also don't trust any government. There's an anti-statism in South African culture which is very healthy for democracy.

This seems to me a very optimistic scenario.

I am optimistic. It's an optimistic scenario based on an understanding of what it's going to take, on the realities of struggle. Democracy at most is the institutionalisation of uncertainty. Utopians will argue that democracy is the institutionalisation of certainty, that everyone will know where they should be, where they're going to get their meal, where they're going to work, how they're going to grow old, and where they're going to recover when they get ill. That Utopia is a recipe for despotism.

But if you accept democracy as the institutionalisation of uncertainty and hence the continuation of struggle, particularly if you retain the independence of civil society from the state, and you accept that the state is a site of struggle, if you thus limit what there is to be optimistic about, then, yes, I think we're going to hold together and we're going to be allowed to continue to struggle. There are an incredible number of intellectuals who have been won over to the social movement and anti-statism. Racism has kept the intellectually gifted in the ranks of the working class, so there is a high-quality leadership at the base.

The ANC is almost like an embryonic state. It's a site of struggle, it's contested terrain. The executive of my branch is three domestic servants, three exiles from MK, and two old-style white lefties, and an accountant in a white suburb. That's the ANC at the base.

22 November 1990.

Chapter 2
Strategy and Tactics: Karl von Holdt and Devan Pillay

The **South African Labour Bulletin** *has since the mid 1970s provided a crucial link between socialist intellectuals and the emergent union movement. Under the editorship of Karl von Holdt it became in the late 1980s one of the main exponents of an attempt to synthesise the workerist and populist traditions within the framework of the Revolutionary Alliance of the ANC, COSATU and the SACP. At the time of this interview Devan Pillay worked on the* **Bulletin's** *editorial team; he now edits the anti-apartheid monthly* **Work in Progress**.

AC: Alex Callinicos; DP: Devan Pillay; KvH: Karl von Holdt

AC: I've been really impressed with and fascinated by the recent issues of the **South African Labour Bulletin**. One of the things that has struck me very strongly is an analogy that pressed itself on me the more I read them. This was an analogy between South Africa in 1990 and Western Europe in the mid 1970s. Both increasingly seem to me situations in which a period characterised by very militant workers' struggle and revolutionary hopes is replaced by a period of at least some degree of reflux, of retreat of shopfloor struggle, and the growth of reformist hopes.

I'm very much aware of the differences in the situations—most obviously, the centrality of the issue of national liberation in South Africa, and the particular circumstance of the whole process of negotiation that's now underway. But, within the working-class movement at any rate, the parallels are quite striking.

First of all, there's a strategic retreat from revolutionary perspectives. I was particuarly interested by your article, Karl, a couple of issues ago, in which you developed an argument drawing on the Eurocommunist reading of Gramsci—an argument relying crucially on the distinction between war of manoeuvre and war of position, very similar to the kinds of arguments that were put forward inside the West European Communist Parties in the mid 1970s, the epoch of Euro-communism—which sought to offer a perspective that was neither social democratic nor revolutionary.[1]

Secondly, there's a shift in economic perspectives away from any idea of replacing capitalism. The kind of ideas coming out of, say, the Economic Trends Group are about somehow reconciling the aim of running capitalism efficiently with that of running capitalism humanely. That again has echoes of the Alternative Economic Strategy that was very influential in, for example, the British Labour Party in the mid 1970s.

The latter was put forward by people like Tony Benn, who did seek to make inroads into capital through nationalisation and so on, but very much believed that state intervention could make British capitalism more efficient and realise some of the demands of the working class movement for higher living standards etc. There were parallels elsewhere in Europe—for example in the French Socialist Party left around Chévènment.

Now that is rather like the idea of growth through redistribution advanced by the ANC and its allies—particularly when you take into account that it's not really growth through redistribution but rather the idea that through promoting growth both of the domestic market and of exports of manufactured goods the material position of workers can be improved. And I'm struck by the fact that some people are talking about a social contract between the working class movement and capital as part of a more general political settlement—which again is very akin to Britain in the mid 1970s.

The third parallel that strikes me is the signs of tension between the leadership of the working class movement, both political and trade union, and at least some rank and file workers. Your reports on the Mercedes dispute are very reminiscent of the kinds of things that happened in the British car industry in the late 1970s.[2] You had then the left of the trade union movement, the Communist Party, which particularly controlled senior shop steward positions, arguing with rank and file workers about the need for wage restraint as part of a strategy of working with capital to run a successful economy.

I was very struck by these parallels, but I have to say that I was also quite alarmed by them. The period in which all these things flourished in the European labour movement proved to be the prelude to a period of very severe defeats for workers—the steam roller of Thatcherism, and indeed in France *Mitterrandisme* rolled over workers' jobs and living standards. Now it's very mechanical to say that history is going to repeat itself in South Africa, but I'd be interested to know what your response is to those observations.

KvH: I don't know that I've got very clear answers to some of the points that you're making. The first thing is just that the analogy with Western Europe in the mid 1970s is a difficult one for me to comment on in any way. I'm not really familiar with the sorts of issues and the sorts of developments that happened there.

Looking at where we are now, there are dangers in the situation, some of which are dangers that you're pointing to—the dangers of what some of us call the 'new realism': either socialism doesn't work or the shift in the balance of forces due to the collapse of existing socialism means that it can't work here and now. So we retreat to a welfare capitalism or social democracy, some kind of conception of the human face of capitalism. I think there is a real danger there.

There are also objective social forces that have been pushing in that sort of direction. There's a coincidence of thinking with the leading forces of capital. The most enlightened wing of capital are definitely seeing that as the option they want to gun for. The Mercedes article makes that clear.

Of course, I think you've got quite a strong temptation within the liberation movement also to think along those sorts of lines. The ANC has been in opposition, in the underground and the resistance movement, for a long time. This rapid transition into dealing with some of the questions of government is finding us, at all levels, totally unprepared and overstretched.

So: what is a realistic economic policy that can take us further towards liberation, whatever we define that as? How big is the ANC Economic Department? Very, very small and very new in a lot of ways. And yet you've got the captains of industry, with their think-tanks, that have got a whole lot of policy studies coming out. That can be quite seductive. And then there's the danger of the new realism coming in with left academics as well, and with the trade union leadership—all of which would point in the sorts of direction that you were talking about.

Now the question that I would want to bounce back is: What does one mean by a revolutionary policy in this period? The article that I wrote on insurrection and 'war of position' was an opening piece in something that needs a lot more work and thinking. But I hope that it's not pointing in the direction of a social-democratic reformism, but that it's actually pointing to the opening up of transformation, organisational bases, and struggles that can take us in the direction of socialism.

One phrase that I would want to look at more closely is the question of establishing bases for socialism in a post-apartheid South Africa. That might be, say, the power of trade unions and organised workers to intervene in and shape economic policy. It might be the organised strength of the unions and workers on the shopfloor to make it impossible for management to manage without worker participation of some sort. Now immediately you raise that you raise the dangers: participation can become co-option, can become absorption into the project of revitalising capitalism. That's where the work has to be done: How do we engage on these terrains without falling into that trap?

It may be a bit simplistic, but one can say: one mustn't abandon the mass action side of the equation. I would think that what happened in Europe in the mid 1970s was that the politics of mass struggle and of taking over institutions and taking over power became relegated to a very secondary aspect of the high-level committees where technocratic decisions were made. You thus saw a shifting of power from the base to the top, and that solidifying into a new form of capitalism.

I don't think this is going to happen here, but it can't just be asserted: theoretical and analytical work needs to be done on a whole range of levels—levels of state institutions, economic institutions, political institutions—to see how you can build your bases for socialism. At the same time, you have to look at the international arena—what your relationship to global capitalism allows and does not allow. One of the ways forward on that is to strengthen the South in its struggle over resources against the North.

DP: All the dangers are certainly there, but I'm also an optimist. There are a lot of exciting challenges for the left ahead of us, primarily because the whole Eastern bloc reference point for most of those who regard themselves as socialists has gone. That has allowed a new creativity to seep in. Many of those who may have been attracted to Stalinist ideas a few years ago are very sincere in accepting the need for creative criticism and non-sectarianism. Others are perhaps so unable to understand what happened in Eastern Europe to be sufficiently aware of what the new agenda is all about. But they are in a minority and don't have vigour and vitality left. You can attack Stalinism anywhere now.

The Communist Party would be that engine room for generating new and creative ideas for the left. It has expressed its willingness to draw in all left forces in the country. And all sorts of unionists from NUMSA and elsewhere have joined the SACP. And it's definitely not the case of these unionists being co-opted. The more I come into contact with the party, the more convinced I am that there is space for that renewal to take place—if people get into the party.

What also strikes me is that amongst the left—the Communist Party, WOSA, any Marxist left the PAC may have, the Unity Movement—there are very few people who are theoretically equipped to be a force to usher in socialism in the immediate term. That's a very sobering observation for us: people want socialism, but they don't understand what it's all about.

You can't talk about insurrection. Insurrection, I've come to believe, is a very dangerous concept in our time. It's loose, and it's irresponsible. If you look at what's happening in the townships, the levels of uncontrolled violence, a lot of youth have guns and are using them for common criminal activities. It's very sobering. The left project is all about equipping ourselves theoretically and moving slowly and strategically in various arenas of struggle.

AC: I'd just like to make a few points here. First, one of the things you were describing, Devan, sounded like a crisis of theoretical understanding within the left. If that exists, it's worth asking what the causes of it were. In my view, the most important cause was the influence of Stalinism and in particular the very distorted conception of the Marxist tradition that it taught people—more specifically, the conception of revolution that it encouraged people to accept, in which the all-knowing party seizes power on behalf of the passive masses.

Now, if there's a failing in theoretical discussion in the **Labour Bulletin** in recent months, it's that it has attended hardly at all to the very powerful strand which I believe is the core of the Marxist tradition. This conceives revolution as self-emancipation, as something which necessarily comes through the self-activity of workers, as necessarily democratic, and for which democracy isn't some kind of afterthought to socialism. Democracy, in the sense of workers' democracy, is constitutive of socialism.

That leads me to a second point. This whole question of insurrection can be presented in a fairly misleading way—which I think to some extent, Karl, you did in your article. So the choice is between either insurrection in the sense of some kind of guerilla warfare conducted by elite military units or this fairly unspecified alternative strategy which involves the use of war of position rather than war of manoeuvre—building up slowly within the existing structures of society.* But it seems to me that within the revolutionary tradition insurrection has been conceived of and even—at least on one occasion, namely October 1917—been practised as something that arises from the collective self-organisation of workers: insurrection is a moment in the expansion of working people's ability to control society.

That leads me to a third point, which is that if you conceive revolution in those terms, that has direct implications for strategy now. Karl, you asked: How do we prepare for socialism now? Well, I think the most important thing is to do everything to promote workers' capacity to organise, their general level of consciousness and political understanding etc. That's where things like the Mercedes affair seem to me very worrying.

Leave aside the rights and wrongs of exactly what happened, which seem fairly obscure despite all the work you did to bring them to light. From a strategic point of view there's something very problematic about union leaders and leading stewards—themselves with a very good history in terms of working class politics—restraining their members in order to arrive at a better

---

*The distinction between 'war of position'—the piecemeal struggle for reforms—and 'war of manoeuvre'—revolutionary struggle for power—is drawn by Gramsci in his **Prison Notebooks**. Eurocommunists in the 1970s argued, mistakenly, that Gramsci believed war of position had *replaced* war of manoeuvre in Western Europe.[3]

arrangement with management and, underlying that, some view about how best to manage South African capitalism. That's precisely the kind of method, as I said earlier, that was used by the Communist Parties, most notably in Italy in the 1970s, with the effect of a catastrophic collapse of working class confidence. This then meant that the Communist Party itself was very exposed when capital decided that it could dispense with its services and move onto a much sharper offensive. So I find the practical implications of the current strategic reappraisal that's going on in the mainstream of the working class movement here very worrying.

KvH: There are quite a lot of different issues involved here. One of the points I tried to make in my article was that a war of position doesn't mean that you ditch insurrectionary tactics and moments, but that you mustn't expect that state power is going to be captured through this moment which is the insurrection. Insurrectional moments and movements have other effects which can strengthen alliance-building, winning of positions and so on, which in turn build the struggle. For example, the peaceful defiance campaigns of the last year were very different from the insurrectionary tactics of 1985-6, but they were in some ways well calculated for the moment, though they held other dangers as well.

So what I'm saying is that it's not just a matter of counter-posing insurrection and gradualism. It's a question of trying to understand the relations between those two things, Power is not going to fall into our hands through an insurrection, as it has been simplistically understood. Therefore negotiations are not to be seen as a poor alternative which necessarily leads to reformism. I don't think people are equipped to handle negotiations theoretically or strategically because they've been brought up on insurrection.

On Mercedes: I don't think that it can be read easily as a case of union leadership imposing restraints on rank and file militancy for the purpose of reaching a better accommodation with capital. It seems to me that an argument can be made for centralised bargaining being a more powerful terrain for the working class to operate on. It's not necessarily simply in the interests of a better relationship with capital, it's something the unions have been fighting for over a number of years as a powerful weapon for building organisational strength and class consciousness beyond the factory and being able to intervene in broader economic and political affairs.

And then once you look at that group of workers in Mercedes, one can't just celebrate militancy, but should ask: What is this particular militancy here? Is the militant rhetoric a cloak for a not necessarily progressive understanding? I'm wary of saying: Militancy means strikes; even better, occupation strike; even better, sleep in; even better, AK-47s on the shop floor. I don't think there's a necessary progression along those lines.

DP: Also it's a question of democracy. Very few people can deny that NUMSA is the best organised and most militant union and has been at the forefront of socialist thinking and struggle. Here you have a section of the workforce—it wasn't the majority—going against national union policy. Why have rules to entrench working class democracy in the union if you say that because there are militants who are on strike, the union leadership shouldn't intervene? I think that's a very dangerous notion.

AC: First of all, on the question of fact: what I took from what Karl wrote was that at least initially, the majority of stewards who were opposed to centralised bargaining, did have majority support, though he gave evidence of them losing it in the course of the dispute. So it seems a little more complicated than how you put it, Devan.

Secondly, national bargaining and what that represents in terms of being able to mobilise workers on an industry-wide basis against the bosses is important. But one of the things that worried me about the whole affair was the extent to which national bargaining became counterposed to the pressure of strong sectional organisation on the shopfloor. Let me illustrate this in British terms. At the height of the shop stewards' movement in Britain in the 1950s and 1960s—which was characterised by a lot of what you've called 'factory tribalism'—in the engineering industry (the metal industry) there were national agreements on pay and conditions, which set a floor, and then the stronger sections of workers would use their power in particular factories to push for better deals. But, rather than strong sectional organisation working against the broader interests of less well organised workers, its effect in pushing up wages and conditions in particular factories was to raise the general benchmark. So you can see there an interaction between strong sectional organisation and national bargaining.

What worried me is that if the priorities of national bargaining are used to snuff out the powerful sectional impulse in particular well-organised factories, you can have the decay of what has been indisputably NUMSA's strength, which is its shop stewards' organisation. That's certainly the historical precedent from the 1970s in Europe that worried me the most. In Italy and Britain, because that was where in the established bourgeois democracies the level of class struggle was highest for the most sustained period, the pursuit of better relations with capital at national level led to a decay of very powerful workplace organisation.

KvH: There are undoubtedly the tensions which you mention. If you take the case of NUMSA, which went into the industrial council for the metal industry in 1983—I think there are big differences between the auto bargaining forum and the metal industry national council. You will find that in many of the factories NUMSA organisation is very weak. Partly this is because they have grown enormously, through central bargaining, and partly it's because they don't have the resources actually to service all those factories. You'll find there are serious complaints in that union and in all the other big COSATU unions, where you have a strategy in the 1970s of focusing on the shop stewards as the spearhead of the union. In some ways that's much less the case now, and that has raised a whole host of problems: to what extent have you got leadership on the shop-floor? To what extent are your organisers in your local offices equipped to deal with what's going on? A lot of the people who've been around for a long time are up there in head office. So you're facing enormous problems of scale, which brings a whole lot of other problems with it.

So the trend you are talking about is created by a number of factors, one of which may be central bargaining, but it's not the only one. The question that needs to be worked on is: What sort of way of institutionalising centralised bargaining can you develop that, on the one hand, does involve people in the plants, and, at the same time, sustains and builds shopfloor militancy and struggles around more immediate issues? I think in different industries there will be different answers. Moses Mayekiso is in favour of dual level bargaining for the engineering industry, which is much what you've talked about. In the auto industry, Les Kettledas of NUMSA is saying: No, it's a uniform industry, there are a small number of employers, dual bargaining doesn't make sense. What you could argue, particularly in smaller industries, is that the progress that's made at the national bargaining forum is going to depend very much on the mobilisation, organisation and involvement in those six companies. Ebrahim Patel suggests in the **Labour Bulletin** that you don't have to have dual bargaining; you can have centralised bargaining that can set different rates for different sectors within an industry or different areas and so on.[4] Then you have the problem that you talked about: you cover the entire industry, there's no room for initiatives at other levels.

The union movement is now facing questions that are much bigger and have much bigger and more difficult consequences than the questions they had to face some years back. I don't know what the answers are. I hope that the thinking in the unions is more advanced than my thinking!

AC: Clearly the thinking that is going on in the labour movement at the minute encompasses more than just the question of bargaining at national industrial level. There's the idea that, just as there are negotiations between the ANC and the regime, there should be bargaining between the organised working class and capital. A lot of people seem to be saying that it's got to be possible to agree some kind of coexistence with capital, which will lead to a long-term strategic advance for the working class, that somehow a stronger position for workers can be institutionalised within the framework of what we all call a post-apartheid South Africa. What are your thoughts about that?

DP: At a certain level that's certainly a strand of thinking, but it's my feeling that the situation is very fluid, on the one hand we are all being realistic about the immediate situation after liberation, or even the situation that's unfolding now. COSATU is participating in the National Manpower Commission. Tentatively, it has forged some sort of relationship with big capital through the struggle over the Labour Relations Act, to the extent that Bobby Godsell of Anglo American spoke of COSATU and big capital being in alliance against the state and said that this argued against the thesis that capital and the state are inseparably intertwined. That trend is going to continue. Sections of capital are eager to forge good relations with the labour movement. The idea of 'participative management' is the big thing now, coming with the Post-Fordism argument that is slowly catching on—looking at the relationship Japanese capital established with its workforce.

But what strikes me is that many people in the union movement are not unaware of this trend. SACCAWU unionists speak of Pick 'n' Pay, Woolworths etc. drawing usually the shop stewards and the more advanced and relatively highly paid sections of the workforce into attractive arrangements at higher salaries. But the unions are very much aware of the flip side, which is casualisation—the denial of rights to, in some cases the majority of the workforce, temporary workers.

Because—unlike in Britain where co-option presents itself much more dangerously—there is a situation of national oppression here, the pressure from the unemployed and the rural areas are very difficult for the unionists to ignore. I talked about us being underdeveloped theoretically, but we have a very mature working class leadership, who are not going to be fooled so easily by anything. This is where the Communist Party comes in—or a party of the working class (it may not be the Communist Party next year). I think they're very much aware of the poverty and dispossession on a wider scale, and about the possibility of creating a labour aristocracy, as in the rest of Africa, where you have sections of the working class being bought off and co-opted into the state. The critical awareness of these issues in COSATU and the Communist Party means that we shouldn't feel too much doom and gloom about the future.

KvH: Well, I' a bit more gloomy. What one is looking at is deeper trends of which the strategists of capital are very aware. There is an awareness, say within the unions, of the kind of problems you're talking about. But if your leadership represents a particular stratum, which does have privileges—high wages, education, etc., and if that stratum's interests become to some extent differentiated from those of a less skilled, lower-paid and unemployed mass, it's very difficult for the leadership to say 'No, we're not going to represent you'. This is especially the case as 'you' are exactly the shop stewards, the full time shop stewards, the regional chairpersons, the presidents etc. etc. of all the unions.

I think that's an element which has contributed to the violence in the townships here. Again in the 1970s, migrant workers and hostel dwellers were often at the forefront, they were the leadership of the unions. They don't exist in the leadership of the unions now. No matter how aware individuals or leadership may be, you've got a danger that willy-nilly what's represented are the interests of a particular kind of elite. So then the question becomes: how do you deal with that? Co-option isn't just a subjective state of mind that happens to some people because they're not aware enough, it reflects a whole lot of much more objective and structural conditions.

On the question of economic policy: as I said earlier, the progressive movement as a whole has been flung into policy-making before it's ready for it. In the case of the union movement, on the one hand, there are certainly overtures coming from capital towards the unions, and you've got unions making counter-overtures. NUMSA, for example, has called for a joint project to shape training for a new South Africa in the metal industry and for the restructuring of the metal industry. But I don't think the prevailing notion of what it means to develop a working relationship with employers is that we can live together happily with capital, that we can have the same interests on these things. I'm sure that it's a danger, but I think there's quite a strong sense that, whatever *lekker* schemes we come up with, these guys are immensely powerful, they've got a very narrow conception of their own interests, and we'll have to fight every inch of the way to get our demands on the agenda.[5]

I think that's a good thing because what it means is that you are going into it in a combative mode. And from that base, unions are all the time negotiating deals with capital. It's not necessarily that different to be doing it at a more national and more economic level—if you clarify for yourself what is the relation between this step and the question of building bases for socialism.

AC: Just on the last point you made: of course, it's true that any serious form of trade unionism necessarily involves making deals, ending strikes as well as starting them. I think the difference is that when you start bargaining about the overall state of the economy, then what you're presupposing is some sort of continuous and institutionalised access by the organised working class to the levers of state power. And at that level, it just seems to me that the historical record is pretty unpromising. There's an enormous experience—again primarily a European experience, so maybe you'd argue that things are sufficiently different here to rule that record out as irrelevant—which shows that attempts to use the organised muscle of the working class to force capital, over a long period of time, to concede policies favourable to the working class have in general ended in failure.

The most sustained example is that of Swedish social democracy, which has collapsed as a strategy. They weren't able to get their wage pacts through the trade unions at the beginning of this year. The Swedish industrialists' organisation has just announced that they're going—ironically, at the very moment when Margaret Thatcher departed the political scene—for full scale Thatcherism. They want to dismantle state intervention, cut down on the welfare state and push the unions out of corporate bargaining. So it's one thing to use the muscle of industrial workers to force concessions from a specific employer or group of employers. It's another thing to believe that you can somehow institutionalise at the level of state power policy-concessions to labour.

DP: I'd be interested to hear what is the alternative...

AC: Well, I laid myself opened to that! One way of putting the alternative is to deal with the question at two levels. First, it seems to me that the response by the left, not just in South Africa but internationally, to the collapse of Stalinism has been essentially to give up on the idea that there is a viable model of socialism that is a real alternative to the market. That just seems to me much too quick, first of all because I believe that Stalinist regimes weren't socialist, so that we shouldn't feel the East European revolutions as a defeat for us, for the left and the working class movement internationally. But secondly, there is a strategy based upon socialist planning that is different from the market or from the kind of bureaucratic command economies that are now falling apart, a socialist planning that in particular would involve an expansion to a national and ultimately international level of the kind of democratic self-organisation that workers currently use to block the power of capital at a workplace level and to force concessions from capital.

Thirdly, the rush towards the market involves, certainly in the West, an enormously rosy eyed picture of what the market's actually like. It probably hasn't happened here to such an extent because—as you know!—the negative side of the market is so obvious in South Africa. But you get this picture of the market as maximising welfare in a way that no other economic system can, which simply doesn't bear any relation to the experience of a majority of people on this planet. So, to summarise, people have just given up on the idea of a democratic socialist alternative to capitalism much too quickly. And this reflects primarily the 50 year old love affair of the left internationally with Stalinism—although you find the same kind of statist approach to the management of the economy in social democracy as well.

The second level of my response is that I don't think it's possible in the long term for a strong, self-organised, militant working class to live amicably with capital. There's such a history of attempts by labour and capital to cohabit ending typically in defeat for the working class—sometimes very catastrophic defeats, sometimes more the kind of slow erosion of confidence and militancy that then allowed capital to go back onto the offensive which I referred to as the West European experience in the 1970s. Sooner or later any strong working class movement is going to have to come to terms with the fact that the only way it can continue to go forward is by a confrontation with capital in which the aim is to replace the existing state with a workers' state.

That doesn't imply a Blanquist strategy of minority insurrection. It does imply that the only way in which workers can entrench their interests is by replacing the existing form of state with one that is organised on fundamentally different lines. So it seems to me that the two things you need to start from are: the possibility and the necessity of a democratically planned socialist economy, and the fact that ultimately revolution is unavoidable, so long as one understands by 'revolution' the classical Marxist conception of self-emancipation, a revolution that comes democratically from below.

DP: I don't want to sound rude, but I come away from listening to you feeling that you haven't said anything, you haven't given us anything to chew on. This is what we all were saying to each other. We all believe in a democratic socialist alternative. We all believe in some sort of revolutionary change. We want a democratic workers' state very different from the present one. But what are we talking about beyond those general ideas? What is the substance of what you are saying? What is a democratic socialist alternative? That is the question you are faced with.

You've capitalism coming with its programme, saying that the IMF and the World Bank will inevitably have to be faced if we want to have the capital to build schools etc. Then you have economists within the ANC coming up with alternatives, but facing the reality of all these dreadful demands and saying: 'Well, there's not much we can do'. We all want a democratic socialist alternative, but we've got to make do with what there is. How do you answer that? That's where I think I'm frustrated with both the Trotskyist left and the Stalinist left. None of them have provided us with anything to really chew on.

KvH: Devan's point concerns the problem of how we conceive of the alternative society. I agree with him: we can talk about democracy, but what does it mean institutionally? How do we organise it? But a second point is, given that we're in a particular situation, in the world and in South Africa, how do we start moving towards the goal of socialism? What strategy of dealing with capital, the state, and the world could be adopted that starts to lead in that direction? I'm hoping that your position can do that. That's why I'd like to know what you mean by a revolutionary perspective in a concrete and immediate sense: how do we deal with the negotiations, those sorts of things.

AC: It's all very well to say: 'I believe in a revolutionary, democratic, socialist alternative to capitalism, but what do we do now?' If you pose the question in those terms, then whatever abstract beliefs you may have about socialism are essentially religious, and what you do in the here and now is governed by quite different considerations. The latter becomes a short-term realism which effectively involves accepting the kind of agenda that predominates within big business and increasingly influences both the ANC and the trade unions. I don't see why we have to accept that agenda. I don't see why socialists have, for example, to construct a viable strategy for South African capitalism, assuming there is such a thing. If you accept that the kind of objective I tried to spell out is desirable, then the objective should condition and shape your practice. You should be judging the initiatives that workers should be taking now in terms of how they contribute to that objective.

I also think that it is possible spell out the objective itself more concretely. Take for example the extremely rich experience of the international working class movement, not just in the developed capitalist countries but also in parts of the so called Third World, of workers' councils, in other words, the forms of political organisation of the working class that emerge out of struggle centred on the workplaces and which represent the beginnings of a very different kind of state from the one we know now. I don't understand why we should ignore that experience. It's something that you can see as recently as the Iranian Revolution of 1978-9, when the workers in the factories built councils—what they called the workers' *shoras*—which represented a real challenge not just to the Shah but to Khomeini and the Islamic Republican Party.

But I come back to the other point I made. One can very easily fall into a kind of schizophrenic thinking where, on the one hand, there are long term objectives, and, on the other hand, there are the immediate realities of the situation, and these immediate realities are governed by the common sense of international capital. Speaking frankly, I'm tired of hearing people say that we have to accept the market as a framework, that the collapse of 'really existing socialism' means that we can't think in terms of a planned economy, and so on. There's a failure of revolutionary imagination and thought that is crippling the left—not just in South Africa but internationally.

DP: As I said, I'm optimistic. I think there is a lot of creativity emerging because the fetters of Stalinism have been removed. The potential is there to build on. But it's got to be outside the framework of traditional Marxist thinking, of both Stalinism and Trotskyism. They remain embedded in the past, in 1917. They can't move creatively beyond that. They are unable to relate creatively to new conditions and new arenas of struggle—for example, absorbing feminist and green elements into their outlook. Both Stalinism and Trotskyism are too authoritarian and dogmatic. If you want to tap this militant creativity of the wider working class and the rural population, the key element is a democratic form of struggle, democratic in its deepest and most meaningful sense. I believe the trade union movement has gone furthest along the road in instilling a democratic culture within the population. The Communist Party has the potential to develop that to wider sections of the oppressed. There is a democratic impulse that exists within the working class, within organisations, that we've got to build on, outside the framework of traditional left thought.

AC: Devan, if I'm guilty of producing abstract generalities, I'm in a contest which you're busily winning. I don't know how useful it is to get into an argument about the relative merits of Stalinism and Trotskyism—though I don't see why the executioners and their victims should be lumped together in the way you do. It does seem to me that dogmatism can take various forms. One form simply asserts that the whole framework of 'left thought' is irrelevant to present struggles without, at the minimum, serious discrimination between the different strands of what you run together under the heading of 'left thought' and sufficient attention to the kinds of experience in those different strands. Dogmatism can take the form of the assumption of creativity.

KvH: I agree with you entirely that there's a danger within the 'new realism' of exactly this uncoupling of the future and present. What happens is that irony and cynicism set in. And that's there, particularly with the post-Stalinists, who've watched their dream crumble, and whose new way of understanding the world is through cynicism: We were young then, we had ideals, now we're realists, we've grown up. That's a very serious problem.

The thing that concerns me is: How do you couple the future to the present? I think there are causes for optimism within the present, there are also causes for pessimism, and a whole series of uncertainties.

What I was hoping to do through looking at war of position was precisely to start exploring the strategy for coupling the present to the future. That's going to entail compromises, but those compromises mustn't be based on an abandoning of the future or a cynicism. There must be an analysis and an understanding of struggle and social development which is capable of laying out how we link the present and its compromises to a future.

This is the problem that I have: how do you link the question of, say, workers' councils with the present and take them into the future? It seems to me to be quite obviously clear that, if you did have the level of consciousness and organisational capacity now to establish a national system of workers' councils, there's a whole series of problems that you'd run into. First, you'd run into the military question and the general arming of the white people and in society in general. You'd also run into exactly the same tendency I pointed to at Mercedes. Whether they're in shop stewards' committees or in workers' councils, the same tendency operates: the professional, full time, activist shop stewards become the experts looking at national questions—the Reserve Bank, exchange rates, techonology deals, etc.—which immediately pulls them out of that militant base.

Then there are other questions. Let's assume that you could confront state power and the power of capital and exist—not replace them as a state, I think it's impossible at this stage. The level of technical, technological, organisational, administrative understanding that you would find within your council framework, that you can find within trade unions, the ANC, or the party, is hopelessly inadequate to run this economy and this state. If you were to start moving in that kind of direction, the investment strike that you could see from big local capital and international capital would be frightening. How do we deal with the consequences of that? How do we deal with the technology problem? The Mercedes plant would come to a stand-still in three weeks if the supply of certain kinds of technology and components were cut off. Are we in a position to replace those? So it seems to me that the scale and scope and complexity of technical, technological, organisational, administrative and political knowledge and decisions really make the vision of workers' councils at this stage just a dream.

Wouldn't, say, COSATU engaging with capital and the state on economic policy and trying to build workers' democratic participation over that be a different way of saying the same thing? That is, provided you conceived of it strategically in a certain sort of way, as trying to build workers' power and workers' access to and control over resources so that we can move in that type of direction. That's why I think Devan's right when he says that talking about workers' councils and other kinds of revolutionary experience doesn't add anything to what we really need.

AC: The difficulty with the sort of strategy you're talking about comes back to the point I made earlier: It's one thing to force concessions from capital in a particular industry or a particular workplace, it's another thing to force long term concessions from capital and institutionalise them at the level of a national economy. First of all, that presupposes, at the minimum, long term influence over the state which I think it's extremely optimistic to expect to achieve. Secondly, everything you say about investment strikes and flight of capital would be as much of a problem for that kind of project. This is shown by the experience, not just of European social democratic governments in the 1970s and 1980s, but also of the Popular Unity government in Chile between 1970 and 1973.

As far as the kind of problems that you argue a revolutionary strategy would face are concerned, I accept that some at least are real ones. I'll just make two points about the capacity of the working class to run an economy as complex as the South African. First, in my experience in Britain—maybe it's different here: you can correct me on that—one of the things that's always struck me is how dependent management are on all sorts of skills and knowledge that workers have but aren't taken into account in the formal structure of how the factories are run. Indeed I've often talked to workers who describe in detail the different ways in which management is incompetent and how they could do it much better. So, while what you say about certain technical problems about components and so on is true, I don't think one should underestimate the existing levels of skills and knowledge workers have.

Secondly, there is the very important point that the very process of transforming society transforms workers themselves. One of the most impressive things about the South African experience is how in a bit over 15 years, a large layer of workers have emerged who have a considerable degree of political and organisational skills. That's in a situation where workers haven't been contesting for power, haven't been, as a class, challenging capital's control over society. Accepting that a challenge for power by the working class isn't on the agenda here and now, I don't see why one can't see that process continuing and reaching higher levels in the future.

The problem of the global economy would be a constraint anywhere in the world. Even the biggest economy, the US economy, is extremely dependent upon international trade for many of the basic electronic components it uses, for example. For me the most important thing here is the international expansion of the working class. The growth of the industrial working class in the so called Third World over the last generation is on a phenomenal scale. Sao Paulo is now the biggest industrial conurbation in the world. The industrial working class of South Korea is of a comparable size to the British. South Africa is part of that experience. And that's not just a question of the number of workers or anything like that, but the growth of the organised working class. Lula got 28 million votes when he stood in the Brazilian presidential elections a year ago. No workers' candidate in the world has ever got that many votes before—in a supposedly backward country.

All this has very important implications. A socialist breakthrough in any country is going to have an international impact by offering a model to workers in other countries which will be a very powerful force. Devan said earlier that Trotskyists are obsessed with the experience of October 1917. I think the international conditions with which the Bolsheviks had to cope were much less favourable than the conditions that we're confronted with today. Even then the Bolsheviks were able to rely on the help of the international labour movement to end the war of intervention against them. So I think that we should look at our sources of strength, both within South Africa and on an international scale, which seem to me very considerable.

KvH: I think that direction is a promising one. There are different ways of building those kinds of relations with militant working class movements in the rest of the world which haven't been developed enough. There's also the sort of capital, in a sense, that we've got in the more reformist trade union movements of the industrialised world.

One very brief point about the question of workers' councils: I don't think how you run production inside a factory is an overwhelming problem. The difficulties have much more to do with how you relate to the rest of the capitalist world outside of the factory—not only in the rest of the world, but in the rest of South Africa: how you administer the factory, how you relate it to other plants, how you get hold of raw materials. These problems are more complex and more difficult. And then there's the question of managing the economy as a whole—these issues become correspondingly more abstract, more general, more complex. And then there are the problems of the educational system, of housing, of the legal system and how to allocate resources between different sectors.

I'm not saying that people can't manage that sort of thing. But they certainly can't manage it now. When you talk about the workers' council type of perspective, that sounds to me simplistic. I would tend to see it as a strand that one can develop with the notion of war of position. I'm not talking about a reformist strategy but one in which your long-term perspective is one of replacing the rule of capital. I think it's quite clear therefore this entails breaking the power of capital within the economy and the state, and that's a rupture of some sort—maybe a series of ruptures, but it's won through the struggle.

If you don't build that perspective into a notion of war of position, no longer what long-term vision you have, you're pursuing a reformist option, in which capital and labour in some sense exist under the overall economic domination of profit. Then for one reason or another, you have a crisis, you have demobilisation, you have capital taking the offensive again, and you're back at square one. There has to be a rupture. One has to develop a perspective which can contain revolution as well as the reformist compromises that are necessary along the way.

What you've had in the past is relatively sudden insurrectionary breakthroughs in very weak social formations, such as Russia, China and Nicaragua. That very weakness dooms the revolution to be deformed, constrains its possibilities. The insurrectionary perspective of workers' councils and so on, which is what Trotskyism seems to stand for—the 1917 vision—is a vision linked to a very weak social formation, where the break can be quite sharp, and then the revolution is burdened with the consequence of backwardness. I think we are in a position to chart a path consistent with the condition of a relatively advanced society. And if we succeed, then we have capital that no other revolution has had.

26 November 1990

Chapter 3

The Communist Party and the Left: Jeremy Cronin

Jeremy Cronin is a member of the Central Committee and of the Interim Leadership Group of the South African Communist Party. Cronin, whose underground activity led to his serving seven years' imprisonment, is also a well-known poet.

It's clear that the East European revolutions have had a fairly traumatic impact on a lot of people in the Communist movement internationally. Probably the best known Communist intellectual in Britain, Eric Hobsbawm, wrote not long ago that those, like him, who had thought the October Revolution had opened the gates of world history had been proved wrong, that the era begun by the October Revolution was over, and that a very profound reappraisal by socialists was needed, particularly by those in the Communist tradition.[1] Now what are your feelings about the depth of reappraisal that's required?

I saw at least one version of the Hobsbawm intervention. I found it very interesting and agreed substantially with what he was saying: in brief, a massive reappraisal is required. Obviously in the South African context there's something of a paradox, which has been remarked upon by quite a lot of commentators, some with a sense of bewilderment! The crisis of the world Communist movement has not impacted on South Africa in quite the same way as it has elsewhere. Here the red flag is beginning to rise up. There's a lot of substantial support for the Communist Party, reflected among other things in opinion surveys (perhaps one of the minor lessons to be drawn from the experience of Eastern Europe is that you should take opinion surveys with some seriousness!).

One observation is that a challenge facing the South African Communist Party is to build on the mass support that we've got, but to build in a way that is healthy, critical, and democratic. If we were to remain simply glib about the support that we've got, we wouldn't actually do service to the socialist project in South Africa. Secondly, following Hobsbawm, we need to explore the different processes opened up by the October Revolution, because that has implications for our party's history which help to explain why, in South Africa in 1990, there is so much support for socialism. The Bolsheviks who made the October Revolution were looking westwards. They saw their own revolution as a holding operation for the generalised red insurrection they expected to break out in Germany, in northern Italy, and so forth. And we know it very nearly did but failed, for a variety of reasons. So the Winter Palace that was seized was seen as merely the first in a series of Winter Palaces, but westwards.

Our party was very much born with that foundation myth—that the western working class was on the brink of making the socialist revolution. That prediction seemed to be nearly fulfilled also in South Africa, in the 1922 Rand Revolt. Here was a very militant class struggle which hoisted the red flag—with funny things inscribed on it!* In South Africa, then, that particular trajectory that was expected failed very evidently, and in a problematic way. That was healthy for the party: it had to reappraise quite rapidly the look westwards and began to realise, from 1924, clumsily at first, that the spearhead of the socialist revolution in South Africa wasn't the white working class.

The Communist Party then found other themes present in the October Revolution—the eastward, southward looking themes of national liberation, which were written into that revolution but were less highlighted, I think, in the original years as everyone was gazing westward. But the party struggled with the connection between national liberation and socialist revolution in the late 1920s and produced a strategic perspective which remains the strategic perspective of the SACP today.

---

*The Rand Revolt of January-March 1922 was provoked by the Chamber of Mines' attempt to weaken the position of white miners by scrapping the colour bar which kept blacks out of skilled work. The resulting confrontation led to an insurrectionary general strike by white workers on the Rand, which the government of Jan Smuts used the army to crush. The infant Communist Party of South Africa supported the strike in the belief that white workers were the vanguard of the broader proletariat, even though the Rand Revolt's most famous slogan was 'Workers of the World Unite and Fight for a White South Africa.'

That perspective was a minority view inside the party in the late 1920s. It was the Comintern that insisted on that particular perspective for the party. The method of its enforcement was to be regretted, and indeed for the next 20 years I don't think the party really understood what it had. Molly Woolton, one of the proponents of the 1928 Theses, by 1930 was arguing that what was envisaged was a federation of independent Native Republics!* There was a very confused notion of what was meant. It was only much later, in the 1940s and 1950s, that a clearer understanding of the richness of that strategic perspective began to be developed.

What I want to come to is the popularity of Communism in South Africa. There are subjective reasons—one of the obvious ones is the demonisation of the Communist Party by an illegitimate, unpopular, minority regime. That produced a lot of emotional support, but that's not something we can rely on when the black-white divisions in our society are less hard-lined. There are also objective factors at play. The crisis of socialism in Eastern Europe, in the Soviet Union and in other parts as well, is a reality which had to be squared up to. But, equally, the huge crisis of capitalism is getting overlooked at present because of Eurocentric and North American perspectives on the global situation. But if one looks at the global situation with the eyes of the South, one realises that socialism has got problems but they are nothing compared with the massive devastation on a global scale that capitalism continues to wreak. The success of capitalism in the advanced countries is directly related to this situation.

Now South Africa presents this global reality in a focused form. Loosely speaking, you have First and Third World cheek by jowl, Soweto and Johannesburg, Guguletu and Cape Town, and so forth. So although Hobsbawm is right that the October Revolution hasn't worked out as expected at all and reassessment is required, maybe there are other trajectories from October 1917 which we are still living out here in South Africa.

*The Sixth Congress of the Communist International, in August-September 1928, led to the adoption of Theses on South Africa which instructed the CPSA (as the Communist Party was known until 1950) to adopt 'the slogan of an independent native South African republic as a stage towards a workers' and peasants' republic.'[2]

I'd like to come back to the relationship between the struggle for socialism and national liberation, which is obviously the central issue in South Africa. But since you've raised the question of the history of the SACP, I'd like to ask you about the whole issue of Stalinism. This isn't because I've got a great desire to hunt for the Stalinist crimes in the SACP's past, but perhaps particularly because of your response to the debate provoked by Joe Slovo's pamphlet **Has Socialism Failed?** *You said that the SACP had been guilty of 'mild Stalinism*[3] *Now, of course, if, as you did, one compares the SACP's record with that of Stalin or Pol Pot, who, I think, were the people you picked out...*

(Laughter) Rather conveniently!

... That's unquestionably true. There's a cheap reply which would be: Well, they had state power, you didn't. But more seriously, I can't say how the SACP operated here in the underground, and I don't want to make any judgements about that. All I can judge is on its performance in exile and in its publications, and there the thing that I'd identify as distinctively Stalinist—apart, of course, from treating the USSR as socialist, which we could argue about—was a tendency to see the SACP as the exclusive embodiment of the South African working class.
I'm thinking, for example, of the kind of hostility that was displayed to the independent unions when they first developed here, which I think is undeniable—a tendency, that is, to counterpose the SACP as somehow objectively the embodiment of the South African working class to the actual struggles and organisation that were emerging inside the country. I think one can call that Stalinist, because it seems to me characteristic of the Stalinist parties that they claimed to be the working class irrespective of what the working class actually did or thought. It's like the famous Brecht poem about the government dissolving the people and electing a new one.
It's clear that the SACP now has a much better claim actually to be the party of the vanguard of the working class in South Africa, given the way the best trade unionists have rallied to the party. But I wonder what your thoughts are about what I've said about the SACP's past and how much you think that's still a legacy you have to worry about in the present.

Perhaps I should begin by saying that I'm not very happy with what I said in the **Labour Bulletin** interview which you quoted. 'Mild Stalinism' is a bit of an oxymoron [laughs], and was perhaps not the best way of talking about the issue. Clearly the party was heavily influenced by its international allegiances, its Comintern involvement and so forth: a shorthand word for that would be 'Stalinism'. What I was trying to say was that although the party may well have supported, without information or understanding, some of the dreadful crimes which took place in the USSR, locally it was not implicated in anything of that level.

But dogmatism, sectarianism, the tendency to be a kind self-proclaimed and eternal vanguard of the working class, all certainly were pronounced tendencies in the party. These were enhanced in particular situations by objective realities. I think exile is a difficult reality for any organisation to live with and to survive. One has to talk very autobiographically: when I came out into exile in 1987, I found that a lot of my comrades weren't particularly interested in hearing what I had to say about the situation on the ground—they wanted to tell me what was happening.

I attributed that less to Stalinism than to the psychological realities of exile. They didn't want things to have changed too much; it was terribly unsettling to feel that vast changes had occured. I think that some of the problems that were perhaps evident in party publications emerging from exile related to that reality—to being cut off, of feeling irrelevant.

Those kinds of experiences tend to produce a certain dogmatism, an abstractness from the realities of the situation. You mentioned one example, the party's fumbling with regard to the emerging trade union movement. The other glaring fumble, I would say, was the emergence of a very vibrant historical materialism, the academic Marxism which arose much at the same time as, and was often interrelated with the developments on the union front. A Marxist party worthy of the name would have been at the centre of that—not by demanding to be the centre, but by becoming the forum, allowing the debate to happen, encouraging it and so forth. The party at best missed all of that, at worst intervened, I think, sometimes in a very sectarian, dogmatic and bad way. I agree with what you're saying. As I say, I would like to stress that this probably had as much to do with the difficulties of exile as with any heavy

Stalinist culture, although I'm sure that too contributed to the problem.

Perhaps another factor that needs to be looked at was that after 1976 there was quite a sharp struggle for dominance. There was no very clear strategic or organisational leadership being provided in the 1976 uprisings. The Black Consciousness movement was, by and large, the dominant force, but it was a very disparate and disorganised movement. What was a pretty spontaneous uprising required organisation. I think, in the course of the 1980s here inside South Africa, in the scramble for organisational dominance and leadership, again there was quite a lot of sectarianism. That applied across the board—so one found it from those with fine Stalinist pedigrees, as well as those without those pedigrees at all.

Certainly from about 1985 onwards the party, I would like to believe, by and large played a constructive role. Some of the support, particularly from the trade unions, that the party is now getting dates back to the mid 1980s, when the party intervened around, for instance, the so called populist-workerist debate by saying: The way forward lies neither through workerism in the narrow sense of economism or syndicalism nor through populism in the sense of class-aligned national mobilisation of the masses. We needed a class perspective, we needed to defend socialism, but also the national liberation struggle was the immediate struggle to be fought. I think that perspective which the party fed in, by and large in a nonsectarian way, particularly through **Umsebenzi**, is partly why we're getting support from people who had been identified as the populists *and* from leading comrades from the FOSATU days who'd been identified as workerists, though whether that was ever accurate is another matter.*

As I say, I don't particularly want to rake over the past...

Perhaps we should!

What I'd like to do—perhaps the past will impinge on it anyway—is to talk a bit about what the implications are of the SACP's critique of Stalinism now, and of what seems to me a fairly

---

*Umsebenzi** is the magazine of the SACP

visible shift in what it says and how it operates. The bottom line of what people like you and Slovo have been saying is that the lesson we must learn from the East European revolutions is that socialism has to be organically wedded to democracy. As a general statement, most people on the left would treat that as unimpeachable.

The problem is that it's a very abstract statement. In particular, there is the question of what is meant by 'democracy', which in turn affects what one means by 'socialism'. If we look at the Comintern tradition, at its founding moment in October 1917, there's a sharp distinction drawn between bourgeois democracy, depending on parliamentary institutions, a passive, atomised electorate, etc., and socialist or workers' democracy which depends upon an active working class that is organised through soviets or workers' councils. At the heart of what I think went wrong with the October Revolution was the decay of the soviets.

Agreed

But it seems to me that there's still a model there of socialist democracy which for a moment at least was realised in Russia and of which we've seen glimpses since, not simply in Western countries—say during the German Revolution after the First World War, Portugal in the mid-1970s—but also during the Iranian revolution—the workers' Shoras which emerged in the process of overthrowing of the Shah. These examples show the model is perfectly consistent with, and indeed couldn't have fully realised itself without, a multi party system. How do you see these different kinds of democracy fitting into the SACP's perspective?

I find no point of disagreement with all of what you're saying at all. The one example you failed to mention was South Africa where I would argue that there were, and are, strong traditions of, not necessarily worker in the narrow sense, but certainly popular, grassroots, democratic organisations like street committees, like self-defence units, like workers' locals, like civics. In the South African context, in a township situation, these approximate often to soviet-type structures. The townships are, with few exceptions, fundamentally working class, and so where those structures have been at their strongest, most vibrant, they've been absolutely dominated by workers. So you don't have to look to 1905 or 1917 for the experience of soviets, it's here. That's the first point.

Secondy, it's not an abstract issue. There is no way that we are going to begin the process of a national democratic transformation of South Africa without very strong local popular organs of the kind we're discussing. That's clearly been one of the problems post-2 February—that spontaneous mass actions and mass organisation have gone onto the back burner a little bit. So it's not some kind of abstract commitment in the first instance to democracy for its own sake or a belief that the longer-term socialist project depends vitally on democracy. Though all of that is true: we're not going to be able to even start the process of change without unleashing those forces on the ground.

That's our strength. What has brought about the alteration in the balance of forces in South Africa—we've not defeated the regime, but there's what Gramsci called a state of reciprocal siege between the liberation movement and the regime—has been mass action and mass struggle. This is not the armed struggle particularly, international isolation to a degree, but fundamentally that reality of mass democracy asserting itself. So democracy is not just our objective, it's our weapon.

Beyond that, I agree with what you were saying. Democracy is a process. Increasingly we see the point that Lenin makes very nicely in **Two Tactics of Social Democracy**—that the same reform measures can have different significance depending on who comes out of that round of transformation with momentum, whether it is the popular masses or an incumbent and reforming regime. We think that the development into the socialist project has the prospect of being pretty continuous with the present democratic phase. There's been a tendency to talk about the democratic phase as opposed to the socialist phase, which is all wrong obviously. Socialism is the deeping of national liberation and the deepening of democracy.

Multi-partyism is not the be-all or end-all of democracy but is an important mechanism and one which we support, for the present but also for the longer-term future. To say the least, the whole question of the commanding heights of the economy is a central issue also in terms of democratisation.

That leads into the question I wanted to raise then about the relationship between the national-democratic and socialist phases, stages, whatever one wants to call them. Going back to what you were saying earlier about the Comintern's orientation on the west rather than the south, I think one of the historic contributions of the Bolsheviks was, as a Marxist party in, for these purposes, a relatively developed country, to assert that the revolutionary socialist movement was a genuinely universal movement, as Lenin put it in his writing on the national and colonial question.

One of the major issues then was how the national liberation struggle relates to the struggle for socialism. What became the canonical formulation in the Communist movement was what is often called the stages theory. Now, it seems to me that there are left and right versions of the stages theory. The right version gives absolute priority to the national liberation stage, and any effort to raise socialist demands and socialist objectives must be restrained for fear of destroying the national-liberation alliance; and there's a history of that having fairly catastrophic results in places like China in the mid 1920s and Iraq in the late 1950s.

The left version is to stress rather what you did—that it's a process, that there's a continuity between the phases of the struggle. That then leads me to two questions. One is that it seems to me as an outside observer that there's been something of a shift in the SACP, from the right to the left version. I'd say five years ago the SACP polemicised quite strongly against people who raised socialism as an immediate question. You're now placing a much stronger emphasis on the socialist aspect of the struggle. I'd be interested to know whether I'm right to detect such a shift, and, if I am, what that represents.

Yes, I think there has been a shift—and shifts are processes too! So no shift is necessarily definitive or watertight. I would also qualify a little some of what you're saying in the sense that your distinction between left and right versions is a little bit mechanical...

Well, there's a element of caricature, yes...

Clearly different conjunctures could require different degrees of emphasis. Some of the earlier emphasis by way of reinforcing the national movement I think was right. Post-1976 one's looking to try and develop a coherent national leadership and a coherent national organisation. I became active in the underground in the 1960s and early 1970s and one read a South African newspaper for a year and never encountered the initials 'ANC', let alone 'SACP'. So there was a real struggle for profile, leadership, coherence, unity and so forth. The ANC succeeded very well in organising the spontaneous revolt of 1976-7, becoming the home of the generation of young militants and revolutionaries which emerged.

From the party's point of view, it read that situation and put its energies into building the ANC. Fundamentally, I believe that was the correct decision. We've got a strong ANC now, spearheading the transformation process from the side of the masses. I think that's not unconnected to particular strategic decisions that party members amongst others took in the 1970s and the first half of the 1980s. They weren't necessarily taking a right-wing perspective on socialist transformation, but were identifying the key organisational tasks—building the ANC and so on.

But I think prices get paid in any strategic decision. I agree with you that in the case of this strategic perspective there was a tendency to underemphasise socialism, even to castigate people who raised the red flag or talked about socialism as workerist or ultra-leftist or whatever. And that certainly lingered on far too long as well. Part of the reason for switching emphasis in the way you're empirically referring to related to developments on the ground here in South Africa. I think the party underrated the mass support, particularly working class support, for socialism. It was underground party comrades working in trade unions and other sectors but also many other left wing comrades who were contributing to the building of a strong and socialist-oriented trade union movement. I think the party leadership woke up a little bit late in the day to what had happened. It was a good lesson. This illustrates a point you were making that to claim to be a vanguard party doesn't mean to say that you are necessarily leading what the hell is going on on the ground.

So from about 1985 onwards, a number of related decisions start to be taken inside the party. One is that the party needs to have a more independent profile. It was difficult to do that, because all our leading party cadres were full time ANC people, many of them at very strategic places inside the ANC, like Slovo. But nonetheless he shifted over and began to work more full time in the party. **Umsebenzi** was launched in 1986 very much to intervene into the new situation. I think from that time you start to see the shift that you're talking about—the processivity of national democratic revolution and socialism, the need to encourage socialist debate and to popularise the cause of socialism. That wasn't an act of disloyalty to the national democratic revolution. On the contrary, in fact.

Given that this shift has taken place, and given that the SACP has now established itself as, without any doubt, the leading political force inside the organised working class, it's not clear to me that you can avoid the kind of dilemmas that confronted what, with a degree of caricature, I called the right version of the stages theory. You described socialism as a deepening of the national-democratic revolution. But it looks as if the decisive moment in the national democratic revolution, in the sense of the transfer of political power, is going to come about through an agreement between the national liberation movement and the existing ruling class. That seems the most likely perspective.
Now that agreement is surely going to be on terms which, even if they conceded the substance of the political transformation—one person one vote in a unitary, democratic, non-racial South Africa, nevertheless are going to involve safeguards designed especially to protect the position of capitalism and therefore precisely to prevent the deepening of the national democratic revolution. So that it may be that we see white domination ended perhaps more quickly than many of us thought or hoped, but that the outcome will take a form that entrenches capitalism and introduces a break where you hope to see a continuity.

Perhaps I could throw the question a little back to you: what safeguards do you see emerging?

Well, I'm sure that you know much more about what's going on than I do, but my own opinion is that the ruling class have made a strategic decision that the only way they can stabilise South Africa is to bring the ANC into government. I think they're probably divided about how much to hedge the ANC in, but I don't think they see an alternative. The ANC is the dominant force among the working class and the youth. The only way they can hope to run this place in a way that will attract capital back is by bringing ANC into government. In other words, they see bringing the ANC into government as a way of saving capitalism in South Africa.

I think that what that's going to mean is insisting that, in exchange for a reasonable majority rule constitution, the ANC only makes very limited inroads into the economic position of capital. After all, there is a model the other side of the Limpopo—that's essentially what Mugabe has done in Zimbabwe. From what I read and hear of the kinds of economic debates that are going on, not simply in the ANC, but in the unions and among left academics, it seems to me that there's a considerable willingness to concede that. Maybe they hope and press for a more humane version of capitalism than exists at present, but they essentially leave the basic structure of South African society alone. That seems to me the problem facing your strategy of deepening the national democratic revolution.

Yes, I agree there's substance in what you're saying. To go back to Gramsci, we're locked in a reciprocal siege. They can't continue in the old way, they recognise this: hence the tactical retreat with a view to occupying a new safer high ground. We are unable to deal the knock-out blow—I think that's a reality. There have been a number of subjective errors and strategic mistakes from the side of the liberation movement, but fundamentally the power equation is complex, and the security forces above all remain a reality behind which, of course, class power rests. So I think one's got to look to the realities of the situation. Realistically, the prospects of substantial economic change in the short term in South Africa are not great—whether deals are struck or not. Apart from anything else we're living in a changed global situation as well, where the possibilities of fraternal support, for any kind of socialist support, have diminished tremendously—not that they were ever that great. So I think one's got to approach impending change with a degree of sobriety.

The political changes which—I agree with you—are fairly likely to occur must be understood not as the national-democratic revolution but as a part of the process of transformation that will continue the present war of position, from which the two major class forces will seek to emerge with momentum. That is the challenge at present facing the two sides. I think over the past few months de Klerk has been winning that process—not irreversibly, but he's certainly scored points in the last year. He's come out with better momentum from the piecemeal changes that have been occuring than we have.

The challenge is to ensure that the extension of democracy in our country becomes a new plateau from which to move forward. That will only happen if the masses are activated in struggle now, if they inform the negotiation process. That's not to say that a very different result will emanate in three or four years' time: whether the masses are mobilised or not, a one person one vote democracy in a roughly unitary system is likely to occur down the line. But if the masses are demobilised, it will enable the capitalist class to consolidate on a new high ground. But if the reverse is the case, if we have a highly activated militant working class making both short and longer term demands, then we have the capacity to keep off balance the regime and the security forces and the capitalist ruling class, and in that way deepen the process of democratisation.

What you've just been saying fits in very closely with the editorial of the latest **Umsebenzi**.[4] *Crudely summarised, what it says is that the popular movement has been quite successful at the level of the negotiating prcess, but has been fairly bad at sustaining the momentum of the mass struggle, and that this is something that needs to be corrected. Is there a sense in which part of the process through which the SACP carves out a more distinctive identity for itself within the Congress alliance is to make itself the organisation of mass struggle, the political force within that broad alliance that is particularly pressing for mass struggle?*

I think there would be a problem if we were to become the sole party of mass action. Certainly we intend to be a forceful voice for that perspective, for mass action. But it would be very problematic for the revolution itself if we were the sole force, out on a limb in this respect. So what we would like to see is a strong ANC-led programme of mass action. I would think we're getting there as well.

What the **Umsebenzi** editorial said was merely repeating what was being said on the ground in a thousand and one ANC branches. The party mustn't become an oppositional force: that would weaken the thrust of the national democratic transformation that's occuring and indeed the socialist project in the longer term. We need to spur the alliance into more effective action.

One last question: sometimes when I look at South Africa at the minute I'm struck by a comparison with the case of Spain in the mid-1970s.

*It was period of intense working class struggle and of political transition from a fascist dictatorship to a parliamentary democracy, in which the Communist Party played a crucial role. The Communist Party came out of the underground with all the prestige of what it had done there, the vanguard party in the sense that the best workers looked to it, were involved in it, and so on, but also undergoing a process of democratisation at least in terms of strategy—witness Santiago Carrillo's famous book '***Eurocommunism' and the State***.*

Now the Spanish CP's contribution to the transition to bourgeois democracy was to prevent the working class militancy that developed from overturning the political apple cart. After that had happened, the CP underwent a precipitous decline, partly because its allies in the political transition no longer needed it, and partly because workers were disappointed by the economic outcome of that transition—they got a battering in terms of wages, jobs and so on. This is a speculative comparison, but do you see any danger of that happening to the SACP—of it being lifted on the wave, but possibly ditched when it's served its purpose?

Yes, I think one shouldn't rule that prospect out. Hopefully there are some important differences in our situation, and hopefully we also learn from history. We should actually be talking about the Spanish and also the Portugese examples of complex transformations from underground, from liberation struggles, into a democratic process, or even about the post 1945 situation in large stretches of Western Europe, where Communist Parties spearheaded the resistance only to find themselves undercut when it came to enjoying the fruits of victory. As a party and as a broad left inside South Africa we need to be familiarising ourselves with all of these realities.

One important difference between our situation and some of the other situations is the character of the alliance between the ANC and the SACP. It's not like the alliance between the Spanish Party and the Socialists. First of all, there's a massive overlap of membership. Second, it's a long alliance. It's a funny kind of alliance. It's not an alliance of two separate forces, but a kind of division of labour within a front of struggle almost.

All of this is obviously related to the racial and national issue in our country, which also means that the kind of stabilisation that capital is looking for is not going to be that easy to achieve in many respects. A kind of bourgeois democratic consensus is more possible in a more stable, culturally uniform, homogeneous situation. Of course, one can look to Zimbabwe and other places, but I don't think the situation is that stabilised there.

It's a nice question. Really what I'm saying is that we should think more in depth about it. Of course, we ask the question in more narrow ways: Are we about to be dumped by the ANC? What happens when it comes to elections? Already, one sees strains of tendency in that direction. There are new people coming on board in regard to the ANC, as one would expect. Last year it carried some risk to belong to the ANC. Now it carries promise. So obviously there are middle strata and aspirant black bourgeois joining, and one would expect from those currents an anti-Communism. But if we do our work properly as a left force, the unions as well as the party, we can ensure that the kind of ANC that is built is not one that easily turns around and breaks us.

If one looks to Zimbabwe, one of the prime lessons I would draw is that ZANU became the bureaucracy, it ceased being a political entity. The fairly weak, rudimentary mass democratic organisations like the workers' organisations and trade unions didn't have an independent vibrancy and were unable to withstand that process, so that essentially ZANU moved from guerila bush force into bureaucracy. I think our reality is different. The ANC's power rests in the civics, the trade unions, the women's organisations, the youth congresses, etc., and rather less in some guerila force which can be disarmed, demobilised and written off, as the leadership transforms itself into a bureaucracy. It won't be that easy for aspirant bureaucrats in our situation. But they will try, of course. One anticipates a struggle in this area, but with some better prospects.

29 November 1990

Chapter 4

Reform in Historical Perspective: Colin Bundy

Colin Bundy is a leading figure in the extraordinary explosion of Marxist thought which took place in South Africa in the 1970s and 1980s. The author of a number of important studies, notably, **The Rise and Fall of the South African Peasantry** *and (with William Beinart)* **Hidden Struggles in Rural South Africa,** *Bundy is currently Professor of History at the University of the Western Cape, where he is involved in the Marxist Theory Group. He is also working on a biography of the ANC and SACP leader Govan Mbeki.*

I think quite a lot of people, myself included, have tended to approach South Africa, certainly in the Botha era, using what one might call the Tocqueville model.* In other words, here is an authoritarian regime attempting to reform and modernise itself to put off revolution. But, for the kinds of reasons that Tocqueville explained in the case of pre-revolutionary France, reform actually exacerbates the situation, both by alienating at least part of the regime's own social base, unleashing a right-wing reaction, and by the fact that every concession stimulates the demand for more, thereby encouraging revolt from below.

Now I think that model fitted, at least as a rough approximation, up to February 1990. It seems to me that we're now in a period where there are less obvious maps by which to chart the process that's now going on.

It's a very intriguing question just to pose it in those ways. I tried in June 1987 to ask in a systematic way whether or not one could

---

*Alexis de Tocqueville was a leading nineteenth century liberal who argued that it was the attempts by the monarchy under Louis XVI to reform itself which unleashed the French Revolution. For example: 'The most perilous moment for a bad government is when it seeks to mend its ways'.[1]

regard South Africa as being in a revolutionary situation. I looked at some of the ways in which people tried to answer that question, particularly at Lenin's very fertile formula. It seemed to me at that time that many of the components of a revolutionary situation—one that Tocqueville would have recognised—were present, with the exception that the South African state never lost, and was never in any danger of losing, control over the forces of coercion.[2]

Now if that way of understanding what was going on no longer applies, how does one even begin to explain it? Are we going to have to make a very big deal of saying 'de Klerk's different from Botha,' and wind up with a totally individuated explanation for the changes? I think that part of an answer would be that probably 2 February, while an important date, was not as pivotal as it seemed at the time.

It may be that May 1988, the indecisive battle of Cuito Cuanavale in Angola, was in many ways as important, or perhaps that it was the shift in the balance of forces in the region that made it possible for de Klerk to happen, for de Klerk's policies to have any purchase.* And then there's 21 March 1990, Namibia's independence—the extent to which there was a package including independence for Namibia, the reforms in South Africa, a ceasefire in Angola, and the withdrawal of South African troops.

It seems to be important to bear all these events in mind, to realise how different it was in late 1989, that for their own reasons the United States and particuarly the Soviet Union were very keen to have a deal. That's very much an international relations perspective, but it does seem to provide what's missing from a lot of analysis of what's happened in South Africa, which detaches 2 February from that larger series of negotiations, particularly the secret meetings between Chester Crocker and Anatoly Adamishin.

---

*The South African Defence Force's failure during an offensive in southern Angola in late 1987 and early 1988, to seize the strategic town of Cuito Cuanavale is widely seen as an important factor in pushng Pretoria to negotiate a settlement in Angola and Namibia. The talks which led up to a final agreement in December 1988 were notable for the involvement of the two superpowers, whose principle negotiators were, for the US, Chester Crocker and, for the USSR, Anatoly Adamishin.

If one's looking for much more deep seated institutional or structural factors behind the kind of leap that seemed to take place in February 1990, I suppose the other one would be the economic constraints that the regime found itself under. It does seem to me that in the late 1980s there was a situation in which international capital, not through some sort of collective decision but through a series of fairly atomistic decisions, essentially said: 'These people can't run a stable society. We're not going to invest or lend them money till there are signs that they can get their act together.' That's clearly connected with the regional shifts, since apparently it was in part the cost of carrying the war in south western Africa that led Botha to negotiate.

Yes, I'm not sure if one could identify a moment at which there was a particular set of pressures which were decisive. It's very clearly suggested by a body of impressionistic evidence that after about 1986 the state and some of its intellectuals became increasingly aware of the salience of the cumulative decision that you were talking of that South Africa was a bad risk. And then I suspect—I don't know how clearly this was perceived—the events in Eastern Europe in 1989 must have themselves contributed even further to the unlikelihood of any significant flow of foreign capital to South Africa.

By 1989 what Harold Wolpe called an 'unstable equilibrium' existed. It was pretty clear that the one side, the South African government, could no longer re-impose control from above. The popular forces arrayed against it had by then realised that they could not seize power from below. As far as the forces led by and represented by the ANC are concerned, the very change in the economy of the ANC, the inability, or reluctance of the USSR to continue as the major bankroller of the military wing of the ANC, must have been a very important factor.

I think the ANC's approach is in many ways easier to understand than the regime's. My own feeling is that for some years the ANC leadership had thought there wasn't an alternative to negotiations, and that the issue was really when would be the most favourable moment for them, whatever the ANC's activists and supporters may have believed.
I think the more interesting question has to do with the regime. In a way it illustrates a problem in historical understanding. The

unstable equilibrium that you referred to clearly had existed at different levels of intensity for some time. Simply on the basis of analysing that kind of impasse, the conclusion that many people drew, including myself, was that it was likely to continue, and that there was no real way that either side could break out of the stalemate. Relative to that analysis, what we seem to have— whatever the background factors—was a kind of creative leap, an attempt to break out of the impasse by seizing the initiative on the part of de Klerk and the people around him, not simply in the state but I assume also in big business as well.

This seems to me to illustrate two points. First of all, history operates by discontinuities, even if they are not revolutionary discontinuities. Secondly, although I don't think that one can reduce history to the creative action of individuals, decisive leadership is important in very delicately balanced conjunctures. One case in point is the way in which, during the transition from dictatorship to parliamentary democracy in Spain in the late 1970s and early 1980s, the very competent team that emerged around King Juan Carlos and Suarez, the Prime Minister, who were prepared to take risks and to defy the military at appropriate moments, played an essential part in the story. It seems to me that the same is true of South Africa.

I'd agree with that completely. But to appreciate what the discontinuity you're talking about symbolised, the moment of discontinuity on 2 February, I think again one's going to have to go back and remind oneself how startling were some of the pronouncements made under Botha. Particularly, there were two phases as I remember it. First of all there was the initial launching of the Tricameral Parliament, where you have that wonderful set of Samuel Huntington justifications for it, and a lot of gobbledegook—cosociational democracy, etc*. People from the National Party government were using the language of the United Nations Declarations of Human Rights, using universal 'liberalist' language to justify what they were doing. Then again in that brief phase between the states of emergency in early 1986 there was another period when under Botha several of his

---

*The American academic Samuel P Huntington was prominent in providing intellectual justifications for the 1983 Constitution, which continued to deny the African majority any say in government.

ministers flirted really quite assiduously with that language, with those notions.

So, yes, you've got the discontinuity that you're properly insisiting on, that level of de Klerk's political intervention. Then you've got the kind of impetus that derives from that moment, the way in which, once having set the thing in motion, it acquired a logic and a force of its own. So you find a wonderful period in February and March 1990 when the leader writers of the pro-government Afrikaner papers had to find a new vocabulary. People who are interested in discourse analysis will find a rich lode to mine there!

So you've got that break, you've then got the momentum that it generated. But I'm also sure that you can't analyse it without going back to look how different the rhetoric and the vocabulary were by the mid 1980s compared with anything before 1976.

Whatever the factors were that prepared for that break—and I think you're right to make 1976 the crucial year: it is more than anything else the struggle in the townships that has forced the concessions, we're on the other side of the divide now. What do you see as the peculiar dynamic of the negotiating process itself?

Clearly there is the relative success that de Klerk has enjoyed since 2 February, and the apparent difficulties that the ANC side has had in directing, controlling, and benefitting from the negotiations process. Certainly it's meant that a lot of very loyal, hard-working rank and file activists have found the last few months quite threatening and quite demoralising. Over and over again they are saying: 'Why are we letting de Klerk make all the running?' Some of that has translated into practical politics in about the last six or eight weeks, with the attempts to re-launch the pattern of mass mobilisation. That attempt has absolutely clearly come from the left. It's been branches, it's been resistance organisations, it's been left-wingers saying: 'We've detached the process of negotiations from what we're good at, from what actually brought negotiations about, from this kind of mass mobilisation.'

To explain this, two sets of factors would need to be identified. One is just the difference in capacity between the two sides. We're talking about, on the one hand, the government of a medium sized industrial state with its civil servants, its university advisers, and everything else. On the other hand we have the ANC, an organisation which has operated very largely in exile for three decades and whose support structures and allies inside the country operated mainly outside the law between 1985 and February 1990. That does mean, I think, in the simplest possible terms, that there's a very real mis-match in the know-how and experience and those kinds of skills.

The other factor is more complicated, and it's to do with what the ANC expects it can get out of the negotiations. You said earlier you thought that the ANC leadership by and large has all along looked to negotiations: I think that's clear. There were elements within the ANC, and we saw some of this at the Kabwe conference in 1985, who were quite genuinely pushing a strategy that was aimed at a seizure of the state.* Whereas, on the other hand, I think the majority position, certainly within the top leadership, continued to look on armed struggle as a way of bringing about a negotiated transfer of power. Now they're in that process at a time when the international conjuncture has made it much more difficult and confusing than it would have been four or five years ago.

A whole set of mooring posts have been submerged, and to an extent a lot of the people involved in negotiating are casting about with depth sounders, trying to work out what waters they are in and where they can safely anchor. There's been a very significant adjustment of expectations, most obviously with respect to nationalisation and other forms of collective owner-ship, and now a fairly robust acceptance of mixed economy, of a reform capitalism.

For me one of the complications is summed up in the word 'normalisation'. This is very much a government word: the government talks about normalisation. I was somewhat alarmed shortly after 2 February when it seemed to me that a lot of people from the ANC and indeed the Communist Party as well also started talking about normalisation. It's a kind of short-hand. It's saying that South Africa's not a normal capitalist society because we've got apartheid and if we can do away with apartheid, then

---

*In June 1985 the ANC held a consultative conference in Kabwe, Zambia, which decided to escalate the armed struggle and voted onto the national executive representatives of the more militant '1976 generation' who had left the country after the Soweto rising.

we become normal—then South Africa would look like any other capitalist society with a bourgeois political framework.

I think that's quite a dodgy assumption to make because of the very peculiar social relations, and power relations more generally that have been generated over the last century since South Africa began to industrialise. A very particular set of industrialising relations of exploitation were hammered out on an anvil of colonial relations of domination. So you've got this extraordinary set of disparities between the possessors and dispossessed, haves and have-nots, employers and workers, whites and blacks. Somehow to imagine that if you fix the political, if you confer civic rights and legal equality, then the whole system will begin to look like Sweden or Denmark seems to me just to be historically very myopic.

What you've just raised very much relates to the long-standing debate about the ANC's and the Communist Party's strategy expressed in terms of the two stages of the struggle—the national liberation stage or the national democratic revolution, and then the socialist stage. Now I take what you're saying to be that that was always bad history—that apartheid and capitalism developed in such a way that the political and legal structures of racial oppression were always very clearly interwoven with capitalist relations of exploitation. However, it may be that, unexpectedly, it will be possible through negotiations to remove those political and legal structures and replace them with those of capitalist democracy. But the effects of a hundred years of apartheid and capitalism aren't going to vanish. Certainly, having just seen Khayelitsha, I find the idea that a simple constitutional change is going to turn South Africa into Sweden is an absurdity.*

It's an obvious point, but one worth mentioning: one looks at Khayelitsha and compares it perhaps with suburban Cape Town. But one must then remember that the creation of Khayelitsha was one of the things that led finally to the abolition of influx control in 1986. Khayelitsha and more generally squatter

---

*Khayelitsha is the vast, wretched urban sprawl which sprang up outside Cape Town in the 1980s to house the influx of Africans fleeing even worse conditions in the rural areas.

settlements and African townships in Cape Town are an expression of how much more attractive that existence is than sub-subsistence in the Bantustans.

So what you're saying is that, appalling though they are, they are a reflection of the failure of the system in its own terms to implement separate development.

I'm saying that. I was also simply adding to the point you were saying. You were suggesting that to see Khayelitsha is to get a glimpse of how difficult it's going to be to bring about real reconstruction directly through legal and political changes. I'm simple underlining that and saying: and even harder to do anything for the *over 50 percent* of Africans living in rural areas.

This all then does take us to the question of the famous second stage, and more generally to the question of socialism. Now one of the many paradoxes is, of course, that socialism in its Stalinist form is dying everywhere, but the South African Communist Party is manifestly a very popular organisation, in particular among militant workers and youth. Two things strike me about this immediately. One is that it's a fairly remarkable story. If one looks at the history of the SACP, it's been able to make the transition from, say, 15 years ago when it was a rather depressed, very sectarian, exile organisation, whose response to the emergence of the independent unions was to denounce them essentially because they weren't the SACP, to an organisation which today has the loyalty of, on the whole, the best people to come out of that movement.

The other point is that in this very difficult transition which is being attempted towards capitalist democracy in South Africa, it seems to me that the SACP is going to play an absolutely pivotal role precisely because it is the organisation that has the loyalties of the shop stewards, the young comrades in the townships, and so on: if the SACP doesn't gain their however grudging consent to the transition, then no-one else is going to be able to. Again the Spanish parallel suggests itself. The Spanish Communist Party was crucial in the mid 1970s in persuading the very militant workers' organisations that had emerged in the previous 15 years or so that they shouldn't press particularly their economic demands too hard. Now it does seem to me that the SACP is going

*to have to play a similar kind of role if there is to be a const-
itutional settlement, but it is a role that will involve considerable
tensions within the ranks of the party and its supporters.*

I think that's absolutely right. The transformation you talked
about is a very significant achievement not of durability but of
the ability to undergo quite real changes. That's not to be sneezed
at. The CP will be 70 years old in 1991, and it's spent four decades
of that entire existence as a proscribed organisation. That it is
once again playing—you call it a pivotal role—at the very least
an important role in South Africa is an intriguing story in itself.
The SACP's ability to transform itself now, the conscious exercise
that it's involved in now of reflecting on its past and, to a degree,
distancing itself from that past, has also another internal
dynamic. That's been the very important exercise of naming the
Interim Leadership, which has meant the incorporation of trade
unionists, of community based activists, and of some
intellectuals.* I would have thought this is quite a dramatic
achievement for the party just in terms of rejuvenation—the
political equivalent of a youth elixir. If one's talking about the
party's demonstrated capacity to respond to changes, I think that
capacity must be enhanced simply by taking new, younger and
more variegated people into the leadership.

*I think that's true, but two things really intrigue me about the
SACP. One is the transformation that they've been able to make,
which, as you say, is quite remarkable and is a tribute to both
their durability and their flexibility. The second thing that
intrigues me is just how they are going to cope with the diverse
forces that they now embrace—very much radicalised comrades
from the townships, workers from unions such as NUMSA who've
come out of the workerist tradition with its emphasis on shopfloor
democracy, a lot of old members who are dyed-in-the-wool
Stalinists of a fairly unreconstructed sort like Harry Gwala.† How*

---

*In July 1990 the SACP announced the formation of an Interim
Leadership Group which extended its Central Committee to embrace
those activists from inside the country some of whom, like Moses
Mayekiso, had not previously been publicly identified with the party.

†Harry Gwala, a long time Robben Island prisoner and leading
ANC-SACP figure in Natal, is perhaps the most vocal defender of the
Stalinist past on the South African left.

*are the SACP leadership going to manage these diverse elements
at the same time as they transform the party itelf? What I see
happening is a transformation from Stalinism to a social
democratic party—probably a left social democratic
party—taking place in a much more concentrated form than it
happened in Western Europe. It's a fairly volatile mixture, isn't
it?*

Jeremy Cronin has written quite interestingly about almost the
problems of success, or the need to get growth right. He talked
about it in terms of building the Communist Party as, at one and
the same time, a mass party and a party of quality. I think that's
an attempt from within the party to address those strains that
you were talking about.[3]

To make a very obvious point: a crucial relationship is going
to be surely that between the party and the trade unions—and
not only COSATU. It'll be very interesting to see whether the
NACTU grouping becomes more militant, whether it also starts
exercising industrial muscle, simply in response to the
expectations of its members because of the talk of transfer of
power. I think that South Africa's in for a continuation of workers'
demands around wages, conditions and so on. I have no way of
knowing whether the party is going to try and lead those, or is
going to try and contain them because of its involvement in the
negotiations and the need for a level of political stability. I would
guess that the relationship between the pressure of increasingly
militant trade union demands—driven both by objective factors,
by the failure of South African capitalism to deliver the goods,
and by subjective factors—and the political leadership of the
South Africa Communist Party is going to be a crucial variable,
possibly the crucial variable.

To use a very obvious analogy, it's the relationship that has
not been achieved in Zimbabwe, where ZANU has blown it with
the unions, and Mugabe is now having to come up with quite a
tough anti-union practice. Now I think that the South African
Communist Party is going to try very hard not to wind up like
that, but it faces a challenge.

*Just from my own conversation with Jeremy Cronin, I'd say that
they're quite clearly aware of the parallel and worried about it. I
suppose it partly depends on—it's a silly way of putting it, but*

anyway—how African a society South Africa is. In a way, this goes back to the question of models: What are the appropriate comparisons to make? Are they with what's happened in the process of decolonisation in the rest of Africa, in some ways culminating in Zimbabwe, which is the closest parallel to South Africa because of its relative degree of industrialisation? Or are the appropriate parallels with more advanced developed western capitalist societies which, like South Africa but unlike the rest of Africa, have powerful working class movements with socialist traditions?

One comparison that some people are exploring, I think quite suggestively, is the one that takes as the model the transition from authoritarian to democratic regimes. Presumably you look not only at Portugal, Spain and Greece, but perhaps especially given the colonial background, at the Latin American states. I would have thought that there probably are, on the political plane, very real comparative perspectives to be gained there. Just hearing you talk a moment ago about the Spanish case reminds me that I should know about it more than I do. I remember some years ago looking at student politics there, and the way in which students and the trade unions linked up in the last Franco years. There were quite startling and, I'm sure, if one pursued them at all systematically, quite fruitful similarities between the way in which student politics constituted itself under Franco and here under the National Party. There's a different trajectory: the trade union movement in Spain is much older and drew more explicitly on the socialist tradition; but you had here a trade union movement much newer, much younger, and much much less theoretically versed in socialism, but actually playing a very strong anti-capitalist role and lining up with student politics in the 1980s.

So I don't think that the African examples are going to tell us very much at all at the political level. There will be points of comparison, I suspect, arising from looking at particular kinds of clientelism. I'm not suggesting that clientelism is peculiar to Africa, but I would bet quite a large sum of money that the whole process of changing the bureaucracy, of going over from that colonial to the swollen post-colonial state is going to happen. So to find a comparison one almost needs to ask in the South African case: Which process are we talking about? South Africa does straddle so many of these categories. Essentially its exports are primary products, but it's also, as you know, an economy that did attain quite a respectable level of self sustained capitalist growth, particularly from about 1948 till 1974. It doesn't absolutely fit into the Spanish or the Latin American or the African pattern, but is going to have points of similarity with them all.

Yes, leaving aside the political urgency of the issues we're discussing, it's precisely South Africa's spanning all these different categories that makes it such an interesting society to study. I'm constantly reminded of Trotsky's concept of uneven and combined development, which, after all, he formulated through his attempts to understand and change a society, namely Tsarist Russia, which also combined features of very developed and very backward societies.

One of the things that is distinctive to South Africa and sets it off from the rest of Africa is the diversity of its Marxist tradition. We've been talking about the SACP, which is the most important strand in terms of influence and so on. But South Africa has one of the oldest Trotskyist traditions, which is still alive, particulary here in the Western Cape, and is reflected in organisations like WOSA, the Unity Movement, and the Marxist Workers Tendency. And there's also the much newer phenomenon of a very vital academic left—all the pathbreaking studies of the 1970s and 1980s.

Both those latter two strands have had some political impact—the academic left through the involvement of many of its main figures in the emergent unions. Do you think there is a continuing contribution that they have to make today?

I'm not sure how dispassionate an answer I can give to that, because in my own practice I would argue and I suppose I would hope—so that there's some reason and some faith involved in my response—that an active left in South Africa which attempts to involve especially intellectuals both from an academic and non academic background seems to me to be one of the things that makes being here very rewarding and possibly, when I look at and read about the experience of left intellectuals elsewhere in the world, sets South Africa apart.

The University of the Western Cape, for example, has a Marxist Theory Seminar which holds very well attended lunchtime lectures, and smaller theoretical discussion groups and reading groups and in September 1991 is proposing to hold a two day conference on the theme 'Marxism in South Africa, Past, Present and Future'. Invitations that have been sent out already to every university in the country, but also to trade unions, to political organisations and to community organisations, have had a very strong, positive response.

Those proposing to hold that conference sent the invitations out to gauge whether or not they would go ahead with the conference, but they now definitely will. As these things go, I think it's quite an important conference, particularly with the shock delivered to even the most confident left academics by the collapse of the particular variety of socialism in Eastern Europe, by the indeterminate fate of Soviet socialism, by the reformulation of some of the objectives of the national liberation movement, by the retreat from Marxism by some academics.

The opening up of the SACP, its version of glasnost, makes more plausible the argument that all the kinds of diverse activities that you were talking about can take place broadly within the political framework defined by the SACP. That does raise the question of whether or not there still is, or should be, a space for Marxist currents independent of the SACP, which, as I have said, have a long history here, and one that from time to time, as you've shown, for example, in the case of people like Tabata and the land question, has made its own contribution?[4]

I'm not sure of this, but I suspect that there are at least two main answers to that. One is going to be the outcome of the climate of *glasnost* that you were referring to for left organisations. There's going to have to be some contestation and some accommodation between that range of smaller, alternative, Marxist groupings on the one hand, and the South African Communist Party on the other. One awaits to see how much contestation, and how accommodation actually takes place.

The second part of my answer goes back to the question you asked a moment ago about debates. I don't think that I'm postulating the free-floating, independent academic, because I don't believe in all of that. But it does seem to me that there's also a role to be played non-organisationally. That is, academics have a role that one can identify, which must surely be their role as intellectuals. They remain responsible for critical thought, for ruthless thought in the sense that Marx used, for not shirking from thinking through all the consequences, even if they're not what you'd like them to be. I think there's an extremely important role for left wing intellectuals in South Africa—to retain that critical discourse. It's not asking them to be adversarial. It is insisting that they sustain a fidelity to their intellectual endeavour. It would be death to left scholarship if that left scholarship were to define its goal simply as a kind of service organisation to the political organisation. I think there has been tensions over the last decade. Some intellectual practice has come pretty close to that role. My own position is to insist, not only on the desirability, but objectively the need for intellectual projects to retain some autonomy of, some critical distance from, some tensions with, political movements.

1 December 1990

Chapter 5
Socialists and the Trade Unions: Moses Mayekiso

Moses Mayekiso is perhaps the most prominent of the new generation of workers' leaders to emerge as the independent unions developed in the 1970s and early 1980s. First a shop steward and then an organiser for the Metal and Allied Workers Union, he was elected General Secretary of the National Union of Metalworkers of South Africa (NUMSA) at its founding congress in May 1987. By then he had been held for almost a year in detention and, with four other leaders of the Alexandra Action Committee, was facing charges of high treason. Their trial stimulated one of the largest international campaigns by the labour movement ever to have taken place, and ended in April 1989 with the acquittal of Mayekiso and his comrades. After his release, Mayekiso, though historically identified with the workerist wing of the union movement, became increasingly associated with the ANC-led alliance and rallied publicly to the South African Communist Party after it was legalised in February 1990. Mayekiso is a member of the Interim Leadership Group of the SACP and President of the Civic Associations of the Southern Transvaal.

How do you see the transition from apartheid to a non-racial democracy that seems to be underway currently in South Africa affecting the prospects for socialism in this country?

I believe that the achievement of national liberation will strengthen workers' resolve to get to socialism. So I don't see a difference between the struggles for national liberation and for socialism. For example, with the present negotiations, the workers through COSATU are formulating policies and programmes. This is not just paper-work but a process of conscientisation of the workers on their demands for the future, which is socialism. There has been a Workers' Charter drafted, which will be the rallying document expressing the aspirations, interests and expectations of the workers in the future, and which they will struggle for whether there is a black or a white government. But these are struggles that were not possible under the apartheid regime and which could be made easier when people have the vote in South Africa. So therefore how we take the current situation is as a terrain of struggle through which we have to pass to get to socialism.

I can see that the establishment of a non-racial democracy will in some way increase the scope of the working class movement to organise and press its demands. But there seems to me a problem: there's the process of negotiations going on between the government and the ANC; and my impression is that there is to some extent a parallel negotiating process going on between the unions and big business, partly as a result of the discussions about labour legislation. What seems to be being mapped out there is some sort of agreement—I've even heard people talk about a social contract—in which the unions are willing to restrain struggle around immediate economic objectives in exchange for capital investing in housing, and in industry and making the economy more competitive to generate growth which then will improve the situation of workers. Am I wrong to see that sort of process going on?

Well, you may be wrong, you may be right, it depends on the determination—on why people are doing those things. Are they doing them, seeing them as an end in themselves—seeing a social contract as an end in itself—or are they like the negotiations that happen on the factory floor, where the trade union negotiates conditions in the factory, where the workers make gains as they go along? If these negotiations are seen as answers, as goals, then that could be a big problem. That would be utilising the militancy of the workers, the militancy of the people. Now we say mass struggles should continue, they should continue even in the future South Africa, when it is controlled by the black people, because you cannot sell the democratic right of people to be able to express themselves. That expression will lead in some areas towards socialism. Mass action, including strikes, stayaways, and boycotts, must be decided democratically by the grassroots constituencies, and not be dictated from above.

My immediate answer to your question is that COSATU has no policy on social contracts or whatever. I think there's just discussions around the issue. In NUMSA we haven't discussed it. So I cannot comment and say it would be a good thing to have social contracts or whatever. It would depend on how such proposals were presented. But the mass struggles have to be conducted. That's what convinces us sometimes to support negotiations. But you must conscientise people, people must know that it's not an end in itself, it's just one of the steps that we have to pass through. You still have to fight for the goal, and use what you get today to get to the end of the tunnel.

I should emphasise that what I've heard hasn't been any question of formal policy about some sort of long term agreement between the unions and big business, but I've been struck by how often people have told me that the idea is floating around. It's clearly at an informal level that this thinking is taking place.

Perhaps I can express one problem about what you've said about the relationship between negotiations and mass struggle, as far as the working class movement is concerned, like this. Obviously at factory level it's necessary to negotiate. Every strike ends with an agreement. It's necessary to come to some sort of compromise with the boss, and that reflects the balance of forces between two sides on the shopfloor. To bargain at the level of the national economy, though, is another thing altogether. Capital has access to far greater levers of power at the national level—they can take money out of the country, they appeal to the state for support in a way which, even under a liberal-democratic regime, the working class can't. So bargaining at the national level between labour and capital seems much riskier.

One particular risk—and here I'm speaking from the experience of countries like Britain and Italy, where we had in the 1970s social contracts or historic compromises between the working class movement and capital—was that, on the whole, unions kept their side of the bargain much better than the bosses, and what that meant was that the unions—at the level of both union officials and shop stewards—had to restrain their own members sometimes from going on strike, which had a demoralising effect upon rank and file workers. So in that case the effect of the negotiations was to weaken the mass struggle and therefore to undermine the strength of the organised working class. This made it easier for capital to go onto the offensive, as it did in Europe in the 1980s with people like Thatcher.

In some periods we have to talk of realities: what can the working class achieve at a given time and in a given situation? There have been struggles in South Africa for years. We are the last part of the continent to achieve national liberation. People have been trying all sort of struggles, and they have gained through those struggles. This makes me think that, given the conditions in South Africa, there's nothing that is going to buy off the militancy or the struggle of the working class. For example, what do you do with the homelessness today? The revolution won't be tomorrow, it will be after 30, 40 or 50 years.

You find that the general theme on the ground is that the trade unions must negotiate. That's why I leave the whole thing to shop-floor bargaining, because trade unions don't just bargain through the officials. There's very serious bargaining on the ground. When you go around and discuss the issue of housing, for example, you find that people think the other struggle is to use your power to gain something, the improvement of conditions in the townships, even through negotiations. There are lots of negotiations going on with the Transvaal Provincial Administration and there could be some successes in some areas and some losses in some areas.

Going back to the question of making compromises with the big bosses maybe at the national level: how do you operate in a situation where, if there are investments, there should be contracts signed by the investors to make sure that such investments are also for needs and not just for profits? What has been exploited more and more is where the investors come in, invest, and take out whatever and however they like. So there should be contracts signed: in Russia you will find Anglo American operating through such contracts. If you deal with international capitalism, then the islands of socialism are not going to work on their own without sometimes co-operation with the capitalist world.

Also what do you do with the internal companies, ones that are owned here in South Africa? Are the workers going to take over those companies? It would be nice if we could do it, but it is not feasible now, assessing the level of our struggles and the power of the bourgeois in this country. So if there's that general mood internationally and internally, don't you have to mix your mass struggle with negotiations, while not forsaking the final goal? Well, I don't have the answers, but these are the questions we are discussing.

I accept that it's a very complicated and difficult situation. All I would say is that there have been very real attempts to pursue this kind of strategy, on the basis of a high level of class struggle, in Europe in the 1970s. For example, when Labour was in government in Britain the left wing of the Labour Party pressed for exactly the sorts of things you were talking about—planning agreements between the government and companies to force the companies to invest productively and so on. It didn't work. Are you saying that it could work here?

What I am saying is that the consciousness of the people is that we want all at the end of the day, but we have to get what we can now, without compromising our final goal. Maybe what happened in Britain is that people felt that the social contract was an end in itself and that they didn't have to struggle any more. There should be short-term programmes—and long term programmes. What is in the Workers' Charter today is mainly short term programmes, because it's difficult to talk of long term programmes, but you have to be clear that we're going to the final goal, which is socialism. But once you have from the beginning those clear-cut lines then anyone making a decision must know that it's on these conditions. Also in the minds of the people it's clear that we're still struggling for our goal. That's why we are insisting on mass struggle. Even if a certain political strategy says 'Don't make mass struggles', the masses are not going to listen to that. The trade union movement, the civic organisations, civil society as a whole, should be watch-dogs, to guard against a sell-out position.

One thing that you've stressed is the importance of being realistic both about what the struggle within the country can achieve and also from an international point of view...

But also still being realistic about what you want to gain, and, when you negotiate, making compromises, but not allowing that to compromise the will to go towards the final goal.

It seems to me clear that the socialist left inside the unions in South Africa, a very powerful force, with a very fine record of leading struggles, building organisations and so forth, has shifted—I wouldn't like to put a time-span on it, but certainly in the last year or so—towards concentrating much more on the achievement of short term objectives, while, as you say keeping your eyes on the future. How much of an influence on that have the events in Eastern Europe had?

It has not been made much of, because the events in Eastern Europe are just recent. But if you take the negotiations at the local level, in the civics, such negotiations have been going on for much longer. And the trade union movement taking up political issues with the bosses, pressurising the bosses to pressurise the government, has been going for some time. There is that tradition in South Africa, where you fight on this side, still talking on the other side, trying to get whatever you can and put that in your pocket and move, to not sit down and say: 'OK, I've crossed the Rubicon'.

Alright, I'll put the question another way. The negotiating process started at a local level and on the shop floor a long time ago. But what influence do you think that the East European revolutions have had on the thinking of the left here more generally.

They have had some influence, because we can't ignore what's happening in the world. The mistakes done in the East have hampered some progress made in some areas in dealing with the problems infesting those societies. But generally people have been aware of those problems. Before the crisis erupted, people were saying that the commandist control of the economy, of politics, and of social issues can't work, and that there should be control from the grass-roots. Hence the independence of the trade union movement and the civic movement from political parties. So people, especially in the trade unions, were aware of all those mistakes and trying to move away from them. So when those problems in Eastern Europe emerged, people in South Africa said: 'Yes, we said so—this can't work'. But it has influenced people to become more resolved that, whether or not we negotiate, politically and economically we must have a different approach to the socialist society.

Sometimes when people reject the commandist economy they say that the alternative is market socialism, in other words, that socialism can somehow be built within the framework of the market. I've seen some articles by people here arguing for market socialism. Do you think that this is a correct response?

Well as far as I'm concerned, the market economy based on the free enterprise system and pure control by the capitalists has not worked. The free enterprise system has not worked in South Africa, it has not worked anywhere in the world, and it won't work in future in building wealth for the people. It will work for the few bosses, but not for the people. You have to have democratisation of the economy, where the workers have a say, if not complete control, of the production process, of production, planning and where the surplus is going. At the same time the government should control investment through investment contracts or whatever, so that the surplus should go to curing the ills caused by capitalist apartheid in South Africa—homelessness, illiteracy, unemployment, disease and the general deprivation of the majority of the people, which are all grave ills in our society. Also the civics must be the watchdogs of democracy in the residential areas to ensure the proper control by the people of whatever happens economically, politically, and socially. If there are such arrangements, there will be a balance of power between the bourgeois and the working class. So, even if we are negotiating today, we should make it possible for the workers to take over control; if they can't take over control now, there should be moves in that direction. That's why the trade union movement and the civic movement become crucial now, more important even than political parties.

Nevertheless, it's surely important for socialists to organise politically as well as to be active in mass organisations like the unions and so on. There has, as you know better than anyone, been an argument in South Africa about what form of socialist political organisation there should be. For example, there was the idea that came up in the early 1980s of some kind of workers' party arising from the unions.
Now, I'm not flattering you to say that you're the best known workers' leader to come out of the independent unions that began to be built in the early 1970s. You're also perhaps the best known

of those to have recently rallied to the South African Communist Party. Do you see that decision as essentially continuing the project of building a workers' party that you began in the 1980s?

Well, as we have been discussing, there is a need for a party for the working class to lead the whole process. The Communist Party is that at the present moment, especially because of the changes that happened and also the way the policies are put forward by the party itself. The general approach is that there should be proper democracy in the party: we should not follow the Eastern bloc situation where there has been a takeover of the trade union movement, of civil society as a whole, the soviets and so on, and instructions come from top to the bottom. The party must be a mass party. It must recruit all those who would like to be identified as socialists, regardless of which kind of socialists they are. It should be the home of socialists, a home where rigorous debates are thrashed out.

The Communist Party is the most supported and the only socialist party at the present moment. The membership of the trade union movement is following the party—I would say 90 percent of COSATU and the youth are in support. This influences the question of whether the SACP should be a mass party. You can't now filter out that mass following inside the country.

There's also been an honest approach to the question of trade union independence: how can the trade unions be independent if the party is organising in the factories? There has been a temporary decision till the Communist Party congress that only the trade unions are organising in the factories. It can have maybe its own education programmes inside the factory, but no decision-making structures. There is still an argument about overlap of leadership between the unions and the party, but we don't know what's going to happen about that.

So all in all my answer is that the party is that workers' party, especially if you look at all the recent developments. Even if there have been doubts in the past, the party has proved itself a workers' party. Therefore it's up to the working class now to democratise the party now that it's above ground. Underground, you couldn't exercise full democracy. Just as in the case of the trade unions, it depends on the working class to make sure that the party fulfils their aspirations and hopes and expectations.

Could you clarify what you said about overlap of leadership?

What I said was there's still an argument about the overlap of leadership: can the leadership of the unions be the leadership of the Communist Party or the ANC? Can trade union leadership be real if there is an overlap of leadership, if the party leaders can be the leaders of the trade union movement and vice versa? There's a great debate in the trade union movement and also in the progressive organisations over that issue at the present moment.[1] All those are interesting debates showing that there is really democratisation, and also that there is going to be control of the organisations, including the party, not by the top, but by the masses, from the bottom, on the basis of debate.

So what you're saying is that the SACP can overcome its past, which even people like Jeremy Cronin acknowledge to have been a Stalinist past, although he says it's a mild Stalinist past. You think the party can overcome that and become a genuinely broad socialist organisation, that it can encompass the kind of democratic tradition that developed inside the unions.

I wouldn't argue on behalf of individuals, because I haven't followed the history of some of the leadership. Talking about the party itself, it has gone a long way already. There's an honesty, where the leadership itself accepts its mistakes. They say: 'We have followed blindly the East's direction, without in some areas seeing the problems, seeing the mistakes, and therefore that has taught us something.' Secondly, the trade union movement that erupted in the 1970s has influenced thinking in the party. Thirdly, the general struggles on the ground in South Africa have contributed to shaping the present thinking. The party has gone a long way to show that it's on the democratic road now that it's above ground.

10 December 1990

Chapter 6.
National Liberation and Socialist Revolution: Neville Alexander

*Neville Alexander is probably the best known Marxist intellectual in South Africa outside the Congress Alliance. While a student at the University of Cape Town in the early 1950s he became active in the Non-European Unity Movement, a grouping of Trotskyist origins which has had a considerable influence on the 'Coloured' intelligentsia of the Western Cape. During a spell of postgraduate research in West Germany at the end of the 1950s Alexander became involved in the Fourth International. After his return to South Africa in June 1961 he broke with the Unity Movement and helped form the Yu Chi Chan Club, which sought to lay the basis of a National Liberation Front to wage a guerilla campaign against the regime. Eventually detained, Alexander was sentenced to ten years' imprisonment on Robben Island. After his release in 1974, he completed a book on the national question in South Africa which he had begun in prison, **One Azania, One Nation**, published under the pseudonym No Sizwe in 1979. With the revival of struggle after the Soweto rising of 1976, Alexander became politically active again, helping to found in 1983 the Cape Action League (CAL) and the National Forum Committee. For many years the Cape Town director of the South African Committee for Higher Education, he is now involved in the National Language Project at the University of the Western Cape. His many publications include **Sow the Wind** (1985) and **The Language Question in South Africa** (1989). In 1990 CAL dissolved itself into the new Workers Organisation for Socialist Action (WOSA) of which Alexander is the chairperson. It should be noted that this interview took place nine months after the others, in the immediate aftermath of the abortive coup in Moscow of 19 August 1991.*

One of the major achievements of Marxism in this country was, starting at the beginning of the 1970s, to develop an analysis of the South African social formation which in particular showed the interrelations between apartheid and capitalism and whose conclusion was that those connections were indissoluble. The concept of racial capitalism, which you in particular have developed, is intended, as I understand it, in part to bring out the fact that those connections cannot be broken and that therefore the only solution to the national question is socialist revolution. Now what I wonder is whether or not that analysis has in your view been in any way undermined by developments since February 1990—in other words, by the apparent pursuit of some kind of non-racial bourgeois democracy by de Klerk.

I think the answer to that is No. I don't think our analysis has changed in essence. I'll come back to it later but I think that the fact that during part of 1990 and of 1991 I spent two semesters at Yale University in the United States has in fact entrenched my view about the correctness of our analysis.

The original analysis of racial capitalism held that racial ideology was one of the main motive forces for capital accumulation in South Africa. In other words, the bourgeoisie in South Africa—unlike, for argument's sake, in Western Europe, where the doctrine of individual rights was an essential part of the ideological justification for capital accumulation—brought about the same effect by utilising racial ideology. Now the historical background for that is, of course, colonial conquest, slavery, and all the rest of it. But the fact is that when, after the mineral revolution of the 1870s and 1880s, capitalism was put on the agenda very clearly in South Africa those pre-existing social relations were transformed in order to maximise capital accumulation and profit in the late nineteenth and early twentieth centuries.

I think there was a tendency—and to that extent we have had to refine our analysis—to see the connection between racism and capitalism as a necessary one. In other words, without racial ideology capitalist development wouldn't have taken place as rapidly as it did in South Africa or wouldn't have taken place at all perhaps. But in essence what we were stressing was the fact that, through the peculiarities of capitalist development in South Africa, racial ideology, racial inequality had become built into the system and that therefore, in order to do away with racism you would have to attack the capitalist underpinnings in South Africa. You couldn't do the one without the other.

Now, since particularly Harold Wolpe's analysis in his little booklet **Race, Class and the Apartheid State**, I think it's become clearer to us that actually we've got to insist on the contingency of the relationship between racism and capitalism. In other words, at certain times racial ideology was and is functional for the accumulation of capital, whereas at other times it could be dysfunctional. So there is no necessary connection, it is a contingent one—I think we all accept that today. This is of course a different thesis from the liberal thesis, which is that racism is allegedly dysfunctional in regard to capital accumulation.[1]

So to that extent the analysis has been refined. But—and this is an irony of history—it was actually your book, **South Africa between Reform and Revolution**, that made it clearer to me personally that the historical, as opposed to the theoretical, link between racism and capitalism in South Africa would make it, I would say, virtually impossible to disentangle racism and capitalism—in other words, to bring about a non-racial capitalist system in South Africa.[2]

I think that what de Klerk is doing, or what any other liberal bourgeois regime would do, is clearly recognising that racism has become dysfunctional, that apartheid has pushed up against all the ceilings that were predicted already in the late 1940s and therefore had to be discarded. That is clear. Any liberal bourgeois regime would have to do that, would have to go back, as I have said in some writing of mine, to the Fagan Commission report of 1947 in which they were promoting the liberalisation of the regime—doing away with pass laws, migrant labour, and so on.[3] So the 'new South Africa' is actually going back to 1948, it's actually pre-apartheid, not the post-apartheid South Africa. Of course, the social structure has changed, the class structure, the level of industrialisation, lots of things have changed, it's not the same country, but nonetheless that decision was made by the white electorate in 1948. Both paths were possible at the time, and both paths, as John Saul and Stephen Gelb pointed out in **The Crisis in South Africa**, could for a while lead to further capital accumulation, to further profitable enterprise and so on, but in the case of apartheid necessarily they would push up against ceilings, and that point came of course in the mid-1960s in South Africa.[4]

So the process that we've seen of moving away from apartheid in a sort of zig-zag way since Vorster's days—under Botha and now de Klerk, who's taken a much more radical stance for obvious political reasons and particularly because of what's happened in Eastern Europe—doesn't however mean that the built-in racial inequalities are going to disappear. On the contrary, the whole point about this is that you do away with the laws of apartheid, you take away the scaffolding, you don't attack the foundations, and the house of racial inequality stands firmly, solidly, on capitalist foundations.

Therefore by deracialising the top, the elite structure at the top of the system, you don't in any way touch the bottom, even if, assuming there is economic growth, there is a general lifting up of the base for the entire population. That doesn't mean that the racial inequality is going to disappear. You're still going to have a situation where for the next 20, 30, 40 years probably, the vast majority of the skilled personnel, the managerial personnel, the capitalist class, is going to be classified white, to go back to their own definitions. The vast majority of the unskilled, semi-skilled, under-skilled, unemployed etc. will be classified black.

As I said earlier, I was confirmed in this view by what I have seen myself in America, which is of course a different situation, but where the power-relations are very similar. The vast majority, certainly proportionally speaking, of the so-called under-class, of the unemployed, of the unskilled are blacks, trapped in ghettos and so on. I think we are in a less favourable position to change that in South Africa unless there is a socialist revolution.

I agree there is an irony in all this, because until February 1990 I did think that they couldn't get rid of apartheid without fatally undermining capitalism in this country. But my view has changed in the past 18 months. Perhaps one way to bring out my disagreement with what you're arguing is to insist on certain distinctions.
It seems to me that we need in the first place to distinguish racial ideology, in other words racism as a way of legitimising certain relations of oppression and exploitation. Certainly racism in that sense, if not gone, is going. Clearly the regime is moving towards

a different way of legitimising capitalist exploitation and so on in this country. They've adopted wholesale the discourse of Western liberal capitalism.

Secondly, and I think much more important, is apartheid, understood not simply as the elaborated form that it took after 1948, but as the whole system of both institutionalised segregation and controls over the movement of black people and the position of black labour within production, all underpinned by white political domination. That for me is what apartheid is. It seems to me that we're seeing the dismantling of apartheid thus understood, certainly inasmuch as it consists in a legal and institutional structure. In that sense it's not really just going back to 1948, because in 1948 they had pass laws, they had a racial franchise, and so on. Those are things that either have gone, as in the case of pass laws, or will go.

Then, thirdly, there's institutionalised racism, which, as you say, is a feature of, not just the United States, but developed capitalist countries generally, but which certainly in the US in particular takes a very pervasive form. I've got no doubt that will continue in South Africa after a negotiated settlement, with a degree of social mobility for some sort of black middle class, which has of course taken place on quite a significant scale in the United States in the last generation. So institutionalised racism will persist in South Africa. But in the US or Britain, socialists fight racism, and it's clear that we're not going to get rid of racism in those countries without overthrowing capitalism. We don't, however, talk about an unresolved national question we have to address. It seems quite important to your argument as I understand it that, because of the effective persistence of apartheid, the national question will therefore remain on the agenda even after the establishment of some sort of non-racial bourgeois democracy, an ANC government, and so on.

Yes, I accept the point you're making except for one thing. Insofar as the capitalist mode of production necessarily generates social inequality, class inequality, that inequality in South Africa is going to continue to be manifested as racial inequality. And that generates a racial consciousness. People don't superficially and intuitively understand that they are at the bottom because they are workers, they understand that they are at the bottom because they are black. And that is what has given rise to the whole national question here, the question of national oppression, the exclusion of people from rights and all the rest of it.

But my point goes further. Insofar as resolving the national question involves the task of unifying the nation, of creating conditions where a unified, if you wish, culture can emerge, to that extent the bourgeoisie in South Africa has certainly failed miserably and deliberately, because creating divisions has been part and parcel of their growth accumulation strategy. To that extent aspects of the national question will remain. The sort of work we're doing on language, culture and more generally education, is necessarily going to continue.

The national question can't be said to have been resolved unless and until there is a clear, national, pervasive sense in which people accept that they are South Africans, or Azanians, to start with, and, secondly, in which people, despite recognising, acknowledging, and respecting the diversity of both customs and beliefs, have a clear allegiance to a common culture. That isn't happening, and isn't going to happen, because of this whole question of racial inequality.

Now I think one of the things that we as socialists have to set ourselves—and something which I have been very critical of in regard to practices of past socialists—is that the oppressed people of South Africa have it in their power to begin to create the conditions of national unity, even now. Take the question of language, a very simple example. There are certain limits undoubtedly, but insofar as we have big organisations like churches, trade unions, sports organisations, and so forth, there are certain things we can actually do.

Socialists have not seen that as a political imperative. They just haven't seen that. Instead, people have been misled by Eurocentrism to the point where the solution has always been posed—and it's a petty bourgeois solution—as 'Learn English'. And of course the people can't, and won't, because, apart from resources, the actual environment for it doesn't exist where they live and speak their home-languages.

But that's only one example. The same thing applies if you look at theatre, if you look at film, if you look at the whole cultural spectrum. And when it comes to education, the kind of demands that we put forward—until the Black Consciousness movement came out with a totally different approach—was always: 'We want the same education as whites.' The idea of a core culture was never promoted as a political imperative, something we could actually do. It was always a negative stance that the movement had.

I'm saying that these issues are part and parcel of our attempt to resolve the national question. The question of extending legal rights to black people, I'm sure, despite what the National Party is now saying in its constitutional proposals, will be resolved within the next generation, and can be resolved within the capitalist framework. There's no doubt in my mind about that, despite the fact that I think it will also give rise to tremendous divisions, tremendous conflict, among whites and even among blacks. But nonetheless that is resolvable, they can find a consociational type of formula in which they can resolve that. They will not have resolved the national question if they do that.*

More an observation first than a question: the other day you drew a distinction between two approaches to the national question. One was what you called the Central European approach, which focuses upon the question of culture. You made me think in particular of someone like the Austro-Marxist Otto Bauer, for whom the national question was primarily a matter of forging cohesion and unity within a particular group that could be understood as national. And then there is on the other hand, I think you called it the Western European approach, which focuses crucially on the question of the state and on political change.[5] Now it's become clear to me from listening to what you say that your approach to the national question is a Central European one. Tell me if I'm distorting what you're saying, but it does seem to me that the issues of language and culture and how those pertain to the unification of a population which is very diverse because of the historical process through which South African society was formed are now, for you, the focus of the national question. Is that right?

Yes and no. Your interpretation is wrong in that I accept, unlike your Central European theorists like Bauer, Renner and so on,

---

*'Consociation', a political system based on the separate representation of distinct communities, has been much discussed by consitutional planners in South Africa since the mid 1970s—about the time that the two states most usually cited as examples of such a system, Lebanon and Cyprus, collapsed.

that the entire population of this country can, and probably will, constitute one nation.

In other words, I'm not saying that the nation is a given phenomenon, an ethnic group. That's the first thing. So there is a territorial state approach to start with. The existing South African state forms the boundaries of the potential nation, not the particular existing cultures.

But—and this is where racial inequality and racial prejudice play such a big part in my thinking—I see no way in which we are going to undermine, reduce, let alone, eliminate racial prejudice and racial division unless we begin to be able to communicate, for example, by a language in the sort of effortless way in which say the English people in England are able to communicate with one another. To do that—and this is very important in our context—it is no good, in fact it would be totally counter-productive, to try to impose a single language, which is what the Afrikaners in some respects tried to do. There has got to be a multi-lingual solution.

That is why we, in the language work we have done, have proposed that people should, apart from their mother tongue, have a good knowledge of English as a *lingua franca*—for the entire population, not only for the middle class, which is what it is for the moment. In addition they should have at least a conversational, or a relatively good, knowledge of a third, regionally important language, so that South Africans, or Azanians, when they meet one another, can communicate easily. There are certain rituals in these things. Any multi-lingual person can tell you that you quickly discover which is the language that the two of you can communicate in best. If I meet a German person, after the first stuttering sentences in English, I know that I've got to speak German to this person, and vice versa. But I can communicate.[6]

Racial prejudice will always be linked to cultural features, like language, like the fact that Bantu-speaking African people tend to speak usually with a particular accent, and that kind of thing. I don't believe that we can simply leave that. The old Unity Movement, for example, literally left all of those things to a sort of, as it were, laissez-faire approach. I believe that language planning is part of socialist planning. It's got to be that in a country as diverse as South Africa.

I wouldn't want for a minute to dispute the importance of the language question and I certainly have read what you've written on the subject with great interest. But isn't the language question one facet of a much bigger problem, which is all the sorts of divisions that exist within the oppressed population in South Africa and within the working class itself? One just has to say the word 'Inkatha' to sum up the political problem it represents.

Now it seems to me that a crucial aspect of overcoming those divisions has to be to forge a much greater degree of working class unity in the process of struggle around material issues. One of the starkest ways in which the ANC-SACP-COSATU leadership have failed their own supporters in the last eighteen months is their abandonment of the terrain of struggle over material questions. For example, NUMSA abandoned their national strike in September 1990 when a struggle over wages could have begun to provide a focus of unity to challenge the sorts of divisions that Inkatha was opening up and exploiting. So although questions like language are important for socialists, it doesn't seem to me that one can deal with the divisions within the oppressed except through a strategy which attaches central importance to the class struggle, the struggle over the material grievances and demands of the masses.

I couldn't agree with you more. The fact of the matter is, as you probably know, we are busy on all these fronts. It's not a question of either/or. I think the immediate class struggle, as you say, is the launching pad for everything else that we try to do. But we've got to think generations ahead of us, literally. You've literally got to think in a country like this two or three generations ahead. It involves in the end material things. The language question, for example, involves, just in the educational sphere, things like textbook production, teacher training. These are huge budgetary problems for a future government. If you have, to take an example, seven Bantu languages (I use the word advisedly) in which you have to produce textbooks, instead of two, which is quite possible, then that makes a difference to what you're going to be able to do.*

I'm not suggesting that the language issue should be given

---

*Like many words in South Africa, 'Bantu' has been distorted by racism. It has, however, a scholarly usage, namely to refer to the main family of African languages in Southern Africa.

the highest priority in our political work. But, as a matter of cultural politics, as a matter of long-term planning, I believe that it's going to be inserted into the programme of action of every organisation, mainly of the intelligentsia, that deal with things like language, for example, teachers and students. You just look at those programmes—you won't find it. And that is what I find so tragic.

Can I now switch the focus of our discussion a bit, to talk about the current situation? Here we are in what is supposedly the 'new South Africa', with rosy prospects of, at minimum, the establishment of a non-racial capitalist democracy in this country. That's supposed to be the agenda of the negotiations, common ground between the two main parties to those negotiations, the government and the ANC. How do you see that whole process developing? Everyone agrees that de Klerk has captured the initiative, that the ANC has to a large degree floundered in response to the state's strategy, and so on. But, beyond that, what do you see as the dynamics of this process?

Well, I've written a lot on this question already, and what has happened has merely entrenched my view on the process. Everyone was starry-eyed at the beginning, especially after the release of Nelson Mandela and others. They expected a smooth, unilinear progress towards a negotiated settlement. It was Cassandras like myself who kept on saying: 'Look, this is one of the most conflictual moments in our history.' And everything that has happened since has confirmed this.

Let's accept first of all that from the right—regardless of what the actual numbers are of those who are willing to take up arms and to undertake terrorist actions and so on—the capacity to destabilise the negotiation process is extremely great. In fact, if opinion polls mean anything, there's no doubt that if the government of South Africa were to hold a white election tomorrow they'd probably lose and that the Conservative Party would probably win, or, if not win, certainly get a very large minority of the seats. Now that indicates a certain level of division which the whites haven't known for decades in South Africa.

Secondly, it doesn't appear as though economic growth is on the immediate order of the day. They don't seem likely to generate sufficient investment capital from both inside and outside the country to pacify whites, to make sure that whites don't lose their jobs, that they don't get insecure about the future of themselves and their children. Growth is the one thing that could, from de Klerk's point of view, rally most of the white population behind him, as well as a large section of the Coloured and Indian population—not necessarily as supporters of the National Party, but as people who had been neutralised, who would support a negotiated settlement if they knew that it meant their jobs and houses are safe. That doesn't seem very likely, in fact the opposite seems the case at the moment.

Then, from the left so-called—where I say 'left' here I mean broadly to the left of the ANC—the Pan-Africanist Congress alone, leaving aside other groups, has a capacity similar to the right to destabilise the negotiation process. One only has to look back at 1960 to realise the determination and the will exist to do that if necessary.* It would be a final resort: I'm sure that no-one in the PAC leadership would even suggest anything like that today. But, if it came to the position where a decision had to be made—'Are we going to get involved in something that we reject in principle or are we going to make a last bid to stop it?'—they'd make the last bid, I've got no doubt about that.

A PAC rally I spoke at recently here in the Western Cape was attended by a very large number of people of whom 85-90 percent consisted of unemployed youth. And that pattern, I think, is beginning to emerge around the country. The militant youth, who determine to a large extent what's going on in townships, tend to support the militants, not necessarily in the PAC, but in the ANC and SACP as well. But as the ANC-SACP gets locked into the negotiation process, the alternative will begin to be seen as being the PAC or even groups to the left of that.

So what I'm getting at is that the idea of a linear progress towards a negotiated settlement without zig-zags, without conflict, without civil strife of a very intense kind, is just nonsense. But obviously the very nature of that process is going

---

*It was the PAC which, as part of its campaign against the pass laws, called the demonstration at Sharpeville on 21 March 1960 which led to the massacre by the police of 69 protesters. Both the ANC and the PAC reacted to their banning during the Sharpeville crisis by launching guerilla campaigns, but the PAC's Poqo was started earlier than the ANC's Umkhonto weSizwe and involved much greater reliance on popular violence as opposed to carefully controlled sabotage.[7]

to inform just how much the whites are willing to concede, because I've stressed in everything I've written that this process is not the result of the victory of the national-democratic revolution—that's a completely wrong way of assessing what's happening or conceptualising the process. It is a decision on the part of the ruling class, specifically the National Party, to undertake a process of reform from above by talking to what they consider now to be valid interlocutors, authentic representatives of the oppressed people, namely the ANC and Inkatha. That, as far as they're concerned, is actually the process taking place. So the concessions are going to be made by them. It is not going to be victories that are going to be scored by the liberation movement. And the extent to which the NP make concessions will depend on the extent to which they believe they've got the capacity to control the situation.

Secondly, one mustn't underestimate the fact that this whole process has been orchestrated so carefully by the Broederbond, that you have got this secret society at the back of everything the National Party is doing.* I would be very surprised, knowing that these people have been listening to people like Samuel Huntington and that he's been giving them seminars on how to undertake a transition to so-called democracy, if they haven't built into their scenarios what I believe is going to happen, namely an anti-apartheid military coup. This will level the playing field and make it possible for them after a few years to hand back power not to the National Party but a non-racial elite.

In other words, you circumvent the entire constituent assembly and the revolutionary potential of that process by clamping on military rule.† The right wing or the left wing will

---

*The Afrikaner Broederbond is a secret society which played a crucial role in the rise of the National Party. Since the NP came to power in 1948, it has acted both as an avenue for patronage within the Afrikaner elite and as a government think-tank. Gerrit Viljoen, Minister of Constitutional Development, and a key figure in de Klerk's government, is a former chairman of the Broederbond.

†One of the main demands of both the Congress Alliance and groups further to its left since February 1990 has been that the new constitution should be drawn up by a popularly elected constituent assembly, rather than emerging from bargaining between the regime, the ANC and others. WOSA in particular has campaigned for one in the belief that the struggle to achieve it could unleash a revolutionary dynamic taking South Africa beyond any capitalist solution.

give you reasons to do so. You can orchestrate it, throw a few vigilantes into the townships or various other things—bomb a few white hospitals or something, and it will happen. The point of military rule will be to deal with the ringleaders among the right and to decimate the left, so that, as in Chile and other Latin American countries, you can then alter the landscape within which capital accumulation can once again take place on a more profitable basis. And it will have the backing of the de Klerks because it's a Broederbond decision, they're all part of that.

I must say that the August 1991 coup in the Soviet Union, even though it failed, confirmed my view that this is the most probable solution in South Africa. It's certainly not the optimal solution for the bourgeoisie, but it's the best they're going to get for the moment. And the West will support that coup, because it's going to be an anti-apartheid coup, it's not going to be a coup to restore the right wing, to restore apartheid. It's going to be a coup to make it possible to deal with the obstacles to a liberalisation of the political economy.

I think that's where we're heading, and I think that's what socialists should prepare themselves for. Although you make hay—to use Pik Botha's metaphor—while the sun is shining, one mustn't forget that if you are having a summer, winter is not very far away. So socialists have got to prepare for that eventuality in any case. All this euphoria about democratic mass organisation is all very well, but if you haven't got something else in your back pocket I think you're going to find yourself pushed back much further than you actually need to be.

This in a way goes back to the change in my view that you mentioned earlier. I never expected the National Party to go even as far as they have. I never expected them to take the risk involved in negotiating with the ANC, precisely because it seemed to me that that entailed the sorts of dangers you've been talking about— destabilisation from both left and right threatening the development of an uncontrollable crisis.
Now I must say what strikes me is that, the NP having taken that gamble, how well it's worked out for them so far. I think that must have something to do with the fact that they took the initiative and moved further than they had to at the time, in February 1990, when the mass movement had been weakened by the Emergency, when they still had overwhelming military predominance, when

*the ANC and SACP were, to say the least, disoriented by the
revolutions in Eastern Europe. By seizing the moment and taking
the initiative, the regime have been able to keep remarkable
control over the situation.*

*I've been struck, first of all, by how weak the far right have been.
I accept that they have a considerable degree of passive popular
support among the whites, but they haven't really been able, as
yet, to do anything serious to destabilise the negotiating process.
De Klerk has been able to get the SAP in particular, probably
against many of its members' own desires and instincts, to move
against the right, most notably at Ventersdorp.[8] I think the far
right is the dog that didn't bark in the night, so far.*

*Equally, the ANC, I think crucially because of the political
weaknesses of their strategy, has really floundered. Of course, as
we know now, the ruthless and carefully directed use of Inkatha
and various special forces—5 Recce and so on—has had a
devastating effect on mass organisation, particularly in the
Witwatersrand.[9] So, you're arguing that the National Party need
a coup in order to remove these obstacles to a negotiated settlement
which, while conceding formal political equality would still
entrench white privilege. As of now, I don't see that they need it.*

I think you're probably over-interpreting me. The optimal
solution for de Klerk and the rulers here generally is clearly a
negotiated settlement in the context of rapid economic growth.
Another of them is undoubtedly a military coup, with the support
of the present government. I have no doubt that the right wing
is going to destabilise the process, and if they don't it's going to
come from the other side, from the left.

The situation in this country is so volatile and the amount
of dying that's already taking place is so terrible that to
destabilise the situation is, in a sense, the easiest possible thing
to do. However, nobody I think wants a coup. I'm of course not
advocating anything of the kind at all. I'm also not suggesting
that the National Party wants a coup. I think if they can
orchestrate this kind of vigilante-type divisiveness and killings
in the townships further without showing their hand, as it were,
they will do that until such time as the ANC is beaten down to
the point where they literally have to accept the worst possible
terms and sell out. Up to now the ANC has had a rag of dignity,
to the extent that they can say: 'Look we're not selling out, we're

simply exploring what the possibilities are. We've suspended the armed struggle, we haven't abandoned the armed struggle, etc., etc.' But the National Party may be able to push the ANC to the point where they will literally be clearly selling out. And at that stage the NP will dictate the terms. I think that's what they actually want.

But it may also be that if the economic situation is so bad more and more whites begin to feel: 'This thing is going to work against our interests. We're going to lose our jobs, our houses and whatnot, education is going to become more expensive. Our children aren't going to have the sort of future we were planning for them'. Then, when a referendum is eventually held, unless de Klerk is exceptionally fortunate, I believe that they might find themselves having to seize power by a coup in order to prevent the results of the referendum becoming public.

Perhaps I could now turn to ask you about the prospects for socialists to the left of the ANC and the SACP. There was after February 1990 this terrific surge of support for the SACP. It certainly seemed that we were entering a situation in which the 'Revolutionary Alliance' of the ANC-SACP-COSATU would be absolutely hegemonic within the mass movement and in particular within the organised working class. Now, because of events within the country, but also because of the hammer blows the Communist Party has suffered from the East European revolutions and the failed coup in the USSR, their hold seems less secure. In the present situation in South Africa—which, I think it's clear from what we've been discussing, is a highly volatile and complex situation—what are the prospects for building a socialist organisation to the left of the 'Revolutionary Alliance'?

Let me make a few points at the very beginning. Ever since the South African Communist Party, I think about three years ago, started saying socialism is not on the agenda in South Africa, we've insisted that socialism is on the agenda. In fact South Africa is one of those countries in the world where the likelihood of a mass socialist movement emerging is greater than in most other parts if the world. We insist on that for reasons, some of which are obvious from our earlier discussion—that the anti-racist response of people to apartheid, to racial capitalism, makes them amenable to the socialist message, makes them amenable to the anti-capitalist movement. We've seen this very clearly in the trade unions, in the civics, in the youth movement, we've seen it all over this country.

So I believe socialism remains on the agenda. But it's become exceptionally clear, especially since November 1989, since the fall of the Berlin Wall, that the international conditions which may have made it possible for us to go to the point of saying that a socialist revolution is on the agenda in the very near future have shifted against us. Therefore any attempt to seize power by the working class is going to be an exceptionally difficult thing to realise at this stage. I don't believe that we can hope in the very near future, say in the next five years, to be put in the position of actually seizing power.

I think for that the military situation, if nothing else, is so loaded against us. The army is still a white army essentially and is really insulated against the revolutionary people by racism. It's not going to be like any other place, like the Soviet Union, Eastern Europe, Iran, the Philippines. The army will shoot if they have to. If they have to mop up people piece by piece while they concede control of certain parts of the country for a while, they'll do it. And they'll have the resources to do so unless there's international intervention, which I don't believe is on the order of the day at all.

So to that extent I think the options that are open to us as socialist groupings in this country are very limited. Obviously the preparedness of the rulers to undertake what they call reform from above does give us political space within which to deploy our own forces and to increase the level of organisation, consciousness, and mobilisation of the oppressed and exploited. I think if it hadn't been for the strategy of the ANC-SACP you would probably have seen a much higher level of those things than is the case at the moment. The masses are being confused and distracted in very many different ways through the kinds of tactics which the ANC-SACP have adopted. You mentioned the way in which they put an end to strikes. We know the same in the educational field. All kinds of diversions are being attempted in order to lower the militancy of the masses.

However, the strategy of mass mobilisation around the material interests of the working class remains a real alternative to negotiations. There is absolutely no reason why around questions of wages, of employment more generally, of working conditions, and of living conditions—the entire civic movement as well as other sectors like education, health and the whole land issue—we shouldn't be in a position to mobilise the people in order to make demands and challenge the realisation of important reforms. That doesn't require negotiations. It doesn't require giving the state a modicum of respectability in the eyes of the people or of the so-called international community. We don't need to get into a class-collaborationist mode at all, and of course as socialists we won't do that.

I believe that the very need of the bourgeoisie to bring about this reform, to restructure the economy, to restructure the political institutions, is a weakness which gives us an opportunity. We could well through mobilisation, through the creation of a united front of all, let's say, anti-collaborationist, anti-negotiations organisations, come to the point, possibly much sooner than we even think, where you will have millions of people in the streets. They could be making the economic and political demands of the working class, and the bourgeoisie will have, as it were, to make the final concession of a constituent assembly. That would still be a bourgeois-democratic solution.

It would be better for them to have a constituent assembly in which they make all the necessary concessions than for the revolutionary masses to ride roughshod over the constituent assembly and sovietise the country. The bourgeoisie know that. They've studied the history as well as we have, and they know that in the final analysis they may have to make that concession. I think they will do everything, including a military coup, to prevent that. But it may well be that, if things move as rapidly as they tend to do in these days, we can find ourselves in that kind of situation.

Whether we'd be able to sustain whatever comes out of that, even a radical-democratic bourgeois government, I have my doubts. Unless the entire thing is internationalised fairly rapidly, I can't see how we'd be able to sustain even that level of democratisation of the polity. So what I'm saying then is that our answer must lie in approaching the entire struggle in this country much more from an international point of view of international linkages—regional, southern African ones in any case. Admittedly we haven't got the kinds of states that you had even say in the Middle East: the southern African states are so dependent on the South African economy that, though they are very important to us, they are not decisive. The decisive partners, as it were, are in Europe mainly. So we need to establish those kinds of relations that will make possible an international solidarity movement of a very physical kind—perhaps like the International Brigades during the Spanish Civil War.

I believe that one really has to think like that again if we are talking about winning socialist victories through the barrel of a gun, as it were. It's not enough for us to hope the army is going to remain neutral or that the white soldiers will throw away their arms and go home. I do think that we've got to think those things through, and not simply get the people into the streets.

You've been emphasising in particular the military strength of the state. Clearly for anyone who's talking about revolution that ultimately is the decisive question. Aren't you, however, overestimating the cohesion of those military forces? There's this classic pattern in revolutionary situations whereby the scale of popular mobilisation begins to disintegrate the repressive state apparatuses. Sections of the armed forces come over to the side of the people and make it possible for the people to arm themselves. We've seen that as recently as the Iranian Revolution of 1978-9. I have talked to Iranian revolutionaries who've described how the people marched on the barracks and almost physically forced the soldiers to come over to them.

Now obviously there's an enormous difference here because of the extent to which the SADF and SAP are dominated by whites. But it seems to me that there are still two points that can be made. The first is that there's been a significant change in the composition of both those forces with the incorporation of larger and larger numbers of blacks. This in turn reflects divisions within the oppressed population itself, but nevertheless in any situation of really intense mass struggle many black policemen and soldiers would begin to re-examine their loyalties.

I remember very vividly during the independence elections in Zimbabwe in 1980 seeing, as the mood of popular jubilation built up because it was clear that ZANU-PF was going to win, black soldiers making all the ZANU signs. These were soldiers who were essentially mercenaries who'd been involved in many of the most brutal atrocities committed by the security forces during the war of liberation.

I don't think that one should underestimate the significance of the change in racial composition of the armed forces in any real revolutionary crisis.

The other thing is that, even as far as the white troops and police are concerned, there is the question of morale. I think it's a dream to think of significant sections of the white repressive forces coming over to the side of a revolution in South Africa. But internal disunity, partly because of the influence of the far right on the SAP and the SADF, demoralisation, giving up the struggle, not seeing the point any more of fighting—I can see all those sorts of things happening to the white forces. So I think maybe you're overestimating the military strength of the state. I think you're quite right to emphasise its importance as an issue, because that's something of which during the risings of the mid 1980s a lot of people were incredibly dismissive. But nevertheless I don't think it's quite as insurmountable a hill to climb as you suggest.

No, I don't think I'm overestimating the problem at all. In fact, what you've just said about the blackening of the army and the police is really part of my analysis. I don't think these people will allow the black component of the SADF to gain critical mass. I think that the racial quota in that army is going to stay for quite a long time. In any case the high command is totally white. At the first sign of mutiny, they'll disarm them and send them home, or lock them up. But that's neither here nor there.

The dynamics of racism is such that in a crisis we will see the most brutal forms of genocide. You don't just use automatic rifles and so on, you bomb whole group areas, ghettos and so on, intimidate the population until they go home. That's what they'll do if it comes to that. Obviously we're now talking of an extreme situation. I don't think that the present cabinet, for example, might find the courage to do that sort of thing. That's why I said earlier that it may well be that, given the need to restructure the economy, they will rather go for the constituent assembly as a last resort. But I really don't think it is justifiable to under-estimate what they'll actually do. You just have to look at the Israelis to know what the hell a racist regime can get up to.

So it's because of all this that I'm so terribly pessimistic about our military capacity. Clearly, as you say, many of the black police and soldiers, even some of the whites, the Bantustan armies, will come over to the side of the people, but these are toy armies, they're not serious in comparison with the rest of the

SADF. So unless there is an internationalisation of the conflict, I believe that our hope for the immediate future rests on the fact that the need to restructure the economy means that they'll go for a constituent assembly option in the final analysis rather than bring about a sovietisation of the situation. And we will then probably be stalled there, unless—and here we are very much in the position of the Russian revolutionaries of 1917—there is an international wave of proletarian revolution. If there is such a wave I think we could go all the way. We certainly would want to go all the way, but I can't see us actually being able to do so in South Africa because of the slave character of the society.

So on the one hand I'm optimistic. I believe that there is an alternative strategy to negotiations, and that we can gain much more in terms of social reform, a real franchise not a qualified franchise and so on, than we would through negotiations. If one looks at it in that sort of opportunity-cost way, then the alternative strategy is actually better from the point of view of all the oppressed, not just of the working class. But on the other hand I'm also pessimistic, because I actually don't see, except through, as I said, an international upsurge of the revolution, how we'd be able to conquer power for the moment.

You talked earlier about making hay while the sun shines, taking advantage of what may, if you're right, prove only to be a slightly more democratic interlude in South African history. However that may be, I think it's clear that one of the problems the movement faces in South Africa is the extent to which the left, in the sense of those people who want to fight both apartheid and capitalism, has been dominated by the SACP and its two-stages strategy. To what extent do you think there's now the possibility of changing that situation through the development of an anti-Stalinist revolutionary socialist organisation?

Well, I think that the major imperative remains for all those on the non-Stalinist left to open up a dialogue, to concert their strategies, in the full knowledge that they disagree with one another. They should try to find those practical issues, be it the question of the united front, be it the question of actions in the trade-union movement, in the mass organisations of the workers, to such an extent that the weight of the left becomes manifest in a more focused manner. It's very dispersed at the moment. You've got people from three or four different non-Stalinist socialist groupings working in COSATU as well as in NACTU in some places, but not concerting. The result is that you go to a COSATU congress and instead of making a real impact on the direction of that congress, people are forced to talk and to vote in different directions. It's completely unnecessary. So I think that's the first thing.

Obviously, where people have decided that the only way they can survive is by an entryist strategy of working in the ANC for example, it becomes very difficult to imagine that on certain crucial issues it will be possible for them to go against whatever the ANC's policy is.[10] But there are numerous important issues—education is one, but particularly in the trade union sphere—where I believe we can and should concert our efforts. I think that unity in action, with some element of strategic collusion, would be a very important starting point. For the medium to longer term, I think that it's becoming actually a luxury for groups that have very little strategic and even ideological differences to keep on fighting one another instead of trying to form larger, more impactful organisations.

Secondly, as regards the position of the SACP, my view is that the result of the coup in the USSR and the banning of the Communist Party of the Soviet Union is going to lead that particular current further to the right. They're going to become a social democratic party. They'll probably end up in the South African context even dissolving themselves and joining the ANC. For them it's really a luxury to have two organisations—they're effectively one organisation. And the few individuals, or perhaps the few hundred individuals, who continue to hold a principled revolutionary position will obviously be expelled or expurgated from the Communist Party. They will probably end up, if they continue politically, within some sort of alliance with other left socialist groups.

Certainly we in WOSA are completely open, as we are open to discussions with any socialist current in South Africa, to having a dialogue with the SACP, either officially or with groups of them who are willing to discuss. We feel that's an important process and that the world-historic situation in which the Communist Party of South Africa finds itself today does give us an opportunity to have a really serious, possibly very fruitful discussion with that party in order to see whether there is another way out. But I do feel that we would probably find ourselves talking to a very small minority, because I can only see the rest moving towards the right. The ANC is locked into what you call the historic compromise from the Italian model, and I think the SACP is going that way. They have no option really, especially after Yeltsin & Co are simply tying the purse-strings and saying there's no more money for the ANC.

Finally, for a mass socialist movement basing itself on independent organisations of workers like trade unions and civics and so on to emerge, certain things must happen in regard to the nationalist movement. Congress, the PAC as well—will need to discredit themselves through the whole negotiation process. And that's not impossible at all. I have no doubt if push came to shove the National Party would humiliate the ANC—if they find that it's in their interest to do so: it's not in their interest at the moment. Once that happens, I think that the possibility of an alternative, radical socialist movement would become a real one.

I don't want to be too strongly influenced by the example of the Brazilian Workers' Party, but I think that, given the existence of different tendencies in the country on the left, it's going to have to be a movement that is extremely tolerant of differences, with a fairly clear short-term programme of action.[11] I think that the united front that hopefully will emerge, no matter what the ANC does, may well be a testing ground for the emergence of such a movement.

The National Forum in the early and mid 1980s I believe had the potential to move in that direction, though of course it was a very different kind of movement with a very specific purpose to it.[12] I think that if the united front is built up around the issue of the constituent assembly, the majority of socialists will find themselves agreeing on the main political issues in the country and having a vehicle through which they can actually promote those interests. So I think that is the best that we are at the moment able to hope for and to work for.

In WOSA itself we believe it's become critical to re-examine the entire socialist project—not in terms of questioning the fundamental principles, but to look at the modalities, to look at even the sort of language that we use in our own country. I think that process of political education about what socialism means, in South Africa, in the world today, what it can mean, what it should mean, is going to be extremely important. I like the German formulation that our socialism, our demands, must really become transparent. People must know not only what we're promising but where it will end. It's not always possible, but it must be absolutely clear to the workers what we're actually saying, rather than these sort of broad, grand slogans that are the mark of propaganda.

We want to be able—when we say that socialism means the most consequential, radical democratisation of our society today, empowerment of the workers, workers' control, etc.—to bring forward very clear demands, for example, about local government or housing, that go in that direction. If these demands aren't there, people will say: 'Socialism is a wonderful idea, it's a wonderful Utopia, but it's not going to happen.' I think that process of education is probably the most important thing that we can undertake at the moment.

9 September 1991

Social Contract or Socialism? The Agenda of the South African Left: Alex Callinicos

Any discussion of the condition of Marxism in South Africa today is confronted by an obvious paradox. On the one hand, the popular constituency for socialism has grown in recent years; the most obvious evidence of this is the mass support enjoyed by the South African Communist Party since its unbanning on 2 February 1990. This is remarkable when set alongside the disarray of much of the western left in the wake of the East European revolutions. On the other hand, an intellectual consensus has emerged on the South African left since February 1990 that socialism is not on the agenda in South Africa. I do not intend in this paper to seek to explain this paradox; rather, I intend critically to examine the two propositions on which this consensus centres. The first is, quite simply, that socialism is not feasible in contemporary South African conditions. The second, which might perhaps be treated as a corollary of the first, is that the best the South African labour movement can hope to achieve in current circumstances is a more humane and efficient version of capitalism. Typically, the project envisaged by the second proposition is assumed to require some kind of partnership between labour and capital—a partnership often summed up by the expression 'social contract'.

I have to say that when I first heard talk of social contracts when I visited South Africa towards the end of last year my blood ran cold. The reasons for this reaction—above all in the experience of the West European workers' movement in the 1970s—will I hope become clear in the course of this paper.

Perhaps this is a good point at which to comment on the contribution that Marxists from outside South Africa like me can make to the development of the left inside the country. Plainly any attempt to prescribe to South African socialists would be both inappropriate and futile. It seems to me, however, that mere uncritical cheer-leading is of as little service to the South African left. One could tell a sorry tale of the Western Marxists who have trailed steadily southwards down the continent in their search for 'socialist' regimes with which to fellow-travel only eternally to be disillusioned. Foreign socialists can make a much more positive contribution. Capitalism is an international system; the experience of the workers' movement is also international. Marxists from other countries can draw to the attention of socialists here what they believe to be the lessons of this experience. It is, of course, for South African comrades to decide how far these lessons apply to their own conditions.

An example of this kind of interaction between Marxists inside and outside South Africa appears when we consider the first of the two propositions I mentioned earlier, which denies that socialism is feasible here. Typically this claim figures as an unargued assumption in contemporary political discussion rather than being explicitly stated and defended. A rare exception is provided by an article by the American philosopher Ronald Aronson.[1] Although I strongly disagree with Aronson's argument I think he has performed a valuable service to the South African left by offering a starting point of debate.

Aronson in fact offers two main arguments against the idea that 'socialism is on the agenda in South Africa'.[2] The first one might be called *the argument from the productive forces*:

> while it is an immensely powerful colonial export economy, South Africa's level of industrialisation is still too low, its level of wealth and culture too low, its black working class still too small and young, the level of urbanisation still too low, to seriously pose the prospect of socialism as Marx construed it.[3]

It is, I think, worth stripping away the inessential features of Aronson's argument. There is, after all, plenty of research which shows that something like two thirds of the African population are effectively urbanised and that South Africa has, by the standards of the 'Third World', exceptionally high levels of proletarianisation, with the overwhelming majority of the population dependent for their subsistence on wage earnings.[4] Even when we set aside these obvious blunders on Aronson's part, it remains the case that the South African economy is a relatively weak component of the global system, still deriving the bulk of its export earnings from primary products such as gold and coal.[5] Surely, then the development of productive forces is too low in South Africa to sustain any attempt to build socialism there?

This is, of course, an old debate, one that has been going on ever since the Russian Revolution of October 1917, and which began between the leaders of the revolution, above all, Lenin and Trotsky, and its social democratic opponents such as Kautsky and Martov. Aronson, referring to this debate, contends: 'History is vindicating not Lenin and Trotsky's boldness in seizing power, but Martov's Marxist caution about needing to wait until the productive forces are sufficiently mature.'[6] Aronson does not, however, confront the arguments for the revolutionary case, especially as they were developed by Trotsky in his later polemic against the Stalinist notion of 'Socialism in One Country'.[7]

Capitalism, Trotsky argued, develops the productive forces on a global scale: it is a world system in a sense inconceivable under previous modes of production. Consequently, even the most developed societies are not self-sufficient economies but rather occupy a (relatively privileged) position within an international division of labour. The construction of socialism depends on the existence of productive forces available only on a world scale. Capitalism, however, proceeds by uneven as well as combined development. Some societies by virtue of their internal contradictions are more prone to socialist revolution than others: industrialising societies such as Tsarist Russia and (arguably) contemporary South Africa are especially politically volatile because of the destabilising impact of rapid capitalist development. But the survival of a revolution, wherever it occurs, will depend on the ability of its makers to spread it to other countries.

The experience of the Russian revolution provides a negative proof of this analysis. Though it was a close run thing, the failure of the German revolution of 1918-23 ensured the isolation of Soviet Russia, and thereby created the conditions of material scarcity which provided the social context for the emergence of the Stalinist bureaucracy.

How well does Trotsky's argument hold up today? At the economic level it seems as strong as ever. The internationalisation of the productive forces has accelerated sharply in the past generation.[8] Even the largest and most advanced economies are highly dependent on the world market: thus the United States imports most of the electronic components used by its industries and in its 'smart' weapons systems, while Japan relies on other countries for most of its raw materials. Attempts by social democratic governments to defy the dictates of international competition have been broken by massive capital flight, most spectacularly in the case of the Mitterrand administration in France between 1981 and 1983.

Two very different political conclusions can be derived from this same experience. One is that it corroborates the kind of strategy defended by Lenin and Trotsky at the time of the October Revolution. The other—which has proved much more popular on the left—is that the only plausible socialist strategy is one which takes place within the framework of the market, rather than one which seeks to replace it. Most famously propounded by Alec Nove in **The Economics of Feasible Socialism**, it is now espoused by Joe Slovo who told the Board of Directors of Woolworths 'socialism and the market are not, as is commonly supposed, opposed to each other in principle. The market is a mechanism for the realisation of value, there is nothing inherently capitalistic about it.'[9]

Perhaps the best way of appraising such a strategy is to consider what, concretely, it would mean in South African conditions, as I do below. Let me first, however, consider Aronson's second reason for denying that socialism is on the agenda in South Africa. This might be called *the argument from the Berlin Wall*:

> Anyone talking about 'the socialist revolution' in 1990, as de Klerk knows only too well, hasn't been listening to the rest of the world. Not only have popular revolutions been undoing many of the historical examples of socialism, but they have passed decisive judgement on one whole model, that of a one-party state which centrally controls most or all of the means of production and sets as its primary task the 'primitive accumulation' Marx saw taking place under capitalism ... It is not just that this and other ideas of socialism have been repudiated: ... those of us inspired by Marxism have become idealists because, 100 years after Marx's death, we have no historically viable example of the alternative we favour.[10]

Now this argument is only at all plausible if we are willing to treat the Stalinist regimes as constituting the main 'model' of socialism. This is, of course, what George Bush and the other leaders of the world bourgeoisie would like us to do and what lies behind their proclamation of the death of socialism. But why on earth should we accept this equation of Stalinism with socialism? In my recent book **The Revenge of History** I offer much more detailed arguments against doing so than I can give here. Very briefly, the Stalinist regimes represented no kind of socialism but rather a particular variant of capitalism, bureaucratic state capitalism. This, as Aronson confusedly gestures towards in his reference to 'primitive accumulation', allowed a number of backward societies to industrialise but, in the context of the increasing global integration of capitalism over the past generation, proved to be a fetter on the further development of the productive forces.

Not simply was Stalinism thus the antithesis of socialism, but a very different 'model' can be found within the classical Marxist tradition. Here socialism is conceived as necessarily democratic, the expansion of the kind of rank and file democracy which spontaneously emerges from working class struggle and its political triumph over capitalist forms of rule. This is the 'socialism from below' celebrated by Marx in **The Civil War in France** and Lenin in **The State and Revolution**. Aronson would presumably dismiss this 'model' on the grounds that it is not 'historically viable'. If he means that no such socialist regime currently exists, that is undeniable: one of the most baleful effects of the influence of Stalinism on the left has been its ability to snuff out new experiments in socialist democracy.[11]

If, however, Aronson is claiming that the classical Marxist conception of socialism cannot be achieved, then that is a proposition which must be argued for rather than merely asserted. In the meantime, it is worth noting that one of the main strengths of the classical view of socialism as the self emancipation of the working class is the way in which it finds a reflection in the best traditions of the South African workers' movement, namely the forms of rank and file democracy which developed in many of the emergent unions in the 1970s and early 1980s.

Instead, however, of exploring ways in which these forms—anticipations of a future socialist society—could be further developed, left thinking in South Africa has come to focus on the search for an alternative capitalist model which would be more favourable to working class interests than the currently prevailing one. This seems, for example, to be the principal aim of the Economic Trends (ET) Group closely associated with COSATU.

An 'alternative strategy' is devised in which the labour movement, in alliance with a sympathetic 'post apartheid' government, could extract from capital investment designed both to enhance the international competitiveness of South African manufacturing industry and to raise the living standards of the masses.[12] As even one member of the ET group, David Kaplan, has observed, the slogan sometimes used to sum up this strategy, 'Growth through Redistribution,' is something of a misnomer, since the strategy envisages that it will be the growth both of exports and of the home market which will make possible improvements in the material conditions of the majority, not the direct transfer of resources from rich to poor.[13] In any case, the thought is plain enough: the aim of the left should be to produce a more humane and more efficient version of South African capitalism.

As in the case of the first proposition, surprisingly few efforts have been made actually to show that this objective is the best that South African socialists can hope currently to achieve. This may have something to do with the intellectual influences on left thinking. The ET Group in particular seem to have adopted wholesale the economic theory developed by the French Regulation School.[14] This is unfortunate, for two reasons. First, the Regulation School's approach is, I believe, inherently defective, as Robert Brenner and Mark Glick have shown in a devastating theoretical and historical critique.[15] Secondly, and more directly to the point politically, the Regulation School concentrates on analysing what it believes to be the differences between various capitalist 'regimes of accumulation'— essentially, ways of combining production and consumption within a profitable framework—and their attendant 'modes of regulation'—the institutions required to stabilise a particular regime.

Crudely put, the Regulation approach is about exploring a historical succession of variants of capitalism. Any idea of tracing the forces driving beyond the capitalist mode of production altogether, let alone of outlining what a socialist alternative might be like, drops out of the picture. It is often claimed as a special virtue of Regulation theory that it accords great importance to the class struggle, but in fact the latter only intervenes to break up an existing regime of accumulation. The capitalist Ruse of Reason then uses the class struggle to help construct a new regime. So, according to Aglietta, the mass unionising drive in the United States during the 1930s contributed to the formation of the new Fordist regime of accumulation which allegedly overcame the Great Depression.[16]

Thus the theoretical tools used by left economists in South Africa predispose them to think of socio-economic transformations primarily as the replacement of one variant of capitalism by another. In any case, the hunt for capitalist models is on, and has taken left economists to some very odd places. Perhaps the most surprising is Bob Hawke's Australia—as if a profligate Pacific Thatcherism presided over by a remarkably corrupt Labour government could have anything positive to teach the South African workers' movement.

In some ways the interest shown by some socialists in South Korea is easier to understand. It focuses on one of the most successful capitalisms of the past generation, whose prodigious expansion of manufactured exports offers a stark contrast with South Africa's inability to break out of its historic position on the world market as a producer of raw materials. It is, however, open to question whether socialists should be seeking to transplant the South Korean 'model' to South Africa. For one thing, it is not clear how socialists who, whatever their other differences, are unanimous in their rejection of command 'planning', can evince great enthusiasm in what is probably the most bureaucratically regulated economy outside what used to be the Eastern bloc. For another, it has yet to be shown how South Korea's rates of growth of output and of exports could be repeated without also copying the high levels of repression which still greatly inhibit the ability of socialists and trade unionists to organise.[17]

Predictably enough, Sweden has figured prominently in the current vogue for capitalist alternatives on the South African left. Sweden has served as Western social democracy's Utopia ever since the 1950s and it is therefore hardly surprising that avowed South African social democrats such as Pieter le Roux should now be trumpeting its virtues.[18] South African discussion of the

Swedish 'model' has, however, failed sufficiently to take into account the following considerations.

First, the success of Sweden under social democratic rule in combining high levels of output, employment and social welfare reflected very specific conditions—in particular, those of a small, export geared economy close to one of the most dynamic areas of world trade, Western Europe.

Quite aside from the question of whether or not some version of these conditions could be repeated in South Africa, there is, secondly, considerable evidence that they no longer hold in Sweden itself. Under the same ferocious competitive pressures which led Sweden recently to apply for membership of the European Community, the employers' organisation, the SAF, launched in November 1990 a five year plan, in the words of the **Financial Times**, 'to destroy the vestiges of the famed Swedish economic model, with its collectivist values of equality and solidarity'. Among the SAF's objectives (all too familiar to a British eye) are the privatisation of state-owned industries, the introduction of market forces into the health service, child day care and old age provision, the abolition of the state-controlled social insurance and pensions systems, the sale of all local authority housing, the introduction of education vouchers, an end to national wage agreements and the state-run wage earners' funds, and the encouragement of employee share ownership.[19] Even if capital is unable to implement this programme in its entirety, its adoption is a symptom of the death-pangs of Swedish corporatism. It would be a bitter irony indeed if the South African left were to seek to embrace the Swedish 'model' when it was disintegrating on its own home soil.

More significant perhaps than theoretical discussion of possible economic models, is the extent to which the idea of regulating rather than replacing capitalism has come to shape the actual policy of organised labour in South Africa. Here the evidence certainly suggests that theory is lagging behind practice. Nicoli Nattrass reports: ' "Social contract" has [become] something of a buzz word. Business leaders often punctuate their speeches with references to the need for a social contract.'[20] The unions themselves have, however, generally been more cautious. Thus Karl von Holdt sums up the discussion at a NUMSA workshop in late 1990:

It might be a good strategy to enter into a 'reconstruction accord' or agreement with a political party which is sympathetic to the working class and likely to become the government. The key player would probably be the ANC, but other political organisations would not be excluded. This would not be a 'social contract' with capitalism but an agreement between unions, civics, rural organisations and progressive political organisations on a national development strategy.

But although an explicit pact with capital is ruled out, the ideas of a 'reconstruction accord' does involve accepting the objective of a more humane and efficient South African capitalism:

NUMSA leadership believes that such a strategy could make the SA economy more competitive in the international capitalist economy. It also believes such a strategy could bring the benefit of more jobs, a greater spread of wealth, increased worker power, and higher wages and increased skill.[21]

The trouble is that making even a reformed South African capitalism work logically entails union leaders working in partnership with big business. And indeed there is already evidence that this is beginning to happen. Last year's Mercedes dispute saw the leaders of the ANC, SACP and NUMSA and the senior stewards at the plant lining up with Mercedes management to defend national bargaining against a majority of stewards supported (initially at least) by the workers themselves.[22] The recent pay settlement between NUM and the Chamber of Mines exchanged better facilities for the union for a wage rise well below inflation, with further increases tied to output targets and the performance of the gold price. No wonder that Anglo's Bobby Godsell, one of the chief business advocates of a social contract, praised NUM for 'taking account of the fundamental pressures on the gold mines' and said that agreement 'structured the relationship between management and union in new and important ways'.[23]

In practice, therefore, long-term collaboration between big capital and organised labour is already taking shape. And what's so bad about that? the open or shame-faced defenders of a social contract may ask. Thus Nattrass contends:

as the eminent Keynesian, Joan Robinson, once observed, there is only one thing worse than being exploited and that is not being exploited at all. Everybody is worse off if there are no jobs and finance available to build houses. Social contracts, in whatever guise, are thus potentially progressive. They force capitalists to recognise the legitimate demands of workers and communities in return for less destructive confrontation. By institutionalising negotiations over key contracts such as the wage contract and the lending contract, the simultaneously conflictual and cooperative nature of such bargains is explicitly recognised by both parties.[24]

Nattrass, like other defenders of a social contract, treats a national pact between labour and capital as a projection of the kind of compromises entailed by collective bargaining in individual workplaces or industries. Now it is certainly the case that every strike involves co-operation as well as conflict with the employer, since it ends in the compromise embodied in the final settlement, a compromise which allows capitalist production to continue. This feature of collective bargaining is not, however, something for socialists specially to celebrate since it highlights the limits of trade unionism, its focus on improving the terms of capitalist exploitation rather than ending it. But in any case, to treat a social contract as wage bargaining writ large is to ignore the much greater variety of resources which capital can call into play on the national arena. The class struggle on the shop floor represents a fairly straightforward trial of strength between the two sides, constantly testing and perhaps altering the balance of forces within a particular plant, firm, or industry. On a national scale, however, organised labour confronts a capitalist class possessing resources—access to the state, control over the mass media, the ability to mount an investment strike—which greatly enhance its bargaining position over questions of long term policy.

The disadvantage under which the labour movement struggles in such circumstances can be confirmed by reference to historical experience. The best comparison by which to appraise South Africa's likely future is not, as social democratic dreamers believe, with Sweden, but with Western Europe in the mid 1970s. A particular combination of circumstances—the onset of the first major world recession since the 1930s, serious political instability (the overthrow of the Heath government in Britain, the decay of Christian Democratic rule in Italy, the disintegration of Francoism in Spain), and an explosion of militant workers' struggles—made the incorporation of the labour movement a prerequisite for any restoration of 'normality'. A willingness on the part of workers' leaders to trade wage restraint for broader political and social advances made possible deals in a number of countries—the Social Contract between the British Trade Union Congress and the Labour government of 1974-9, the 'historic compromise' offered by the Italian Communist Party to Christian Democracy and the Moncloa Pact struck between the Suarez government and the Spanish employers' and workers' organisations in 1977.

In none of these cases was the outcome 'more jobs, a greater spread of wealth, increased workers' power, and higher wages and increased skills'. The union leaders generally kept their side of the bargain: wage increases were held below the rate of inflation. The impact of cuts in real wages and accelerating unemployment—the workers' sacrificies did not save jobs—was to create widespread demoralisation and apathy among the rank and file of the labour movement.

The trade union and political leadership of the workers' movement found itself increasingly isolated from the shopfloor. The beginning of the decline of the Italian and the Spanish Communist Parties can be dated from this period. Once the workers' militancy of the early and mid 1970s had thus been diffused, it became possible for the employers to adopt a more confrontational strategy which took advantage of the erosion of workplace organisation. The most spectacular example of such a shift came in Britain when the Social Contract gave way to Thatcherism, but there are other cases—for example, the mass sacking by Fiat of militants in 1980.[25]

This experience suggests that while it is possible for the workers' movement to wrest concessions from the employers either individually or collectively such as higher wages and improved welfare services, winning control or even substantial influence over matters of long term policy is, except in highly unusual circumstances, impossible in a capitalist context. The promise of such control or influence may, however, be highly effective in containing proletarian insurgency. This is particular so because immediate reductions in living standards which are accepted in the hope of grand political objectives help undermine rank and file organisation where it matters most, in the workplace. If this analysis is correct, then social contracts should be avoided like the plague.

One response defenders of a social contact might make is to deny the relevance of the West European circumstances of the 1970s to contemporary South Africa, which is, after all, not a developed capitalist country like Britain or Italy. In this case they would have to explain why it is appropriate for them to invoke such cases as Sweden or Australia in order to justify the sort of strategy they are pursuing.

More seriously, however, what are the real differences which mean that a South African social contract could avoid the disasters of Britain or Italy in the 1970s? Two spring to mind. One is that the South African labour movement may be able to count on a far more sympathetic government than their West European counterparts could. NUMSA, according to von Holdt, envisages, as we have seen, an 'accord' between COSATU and the ANC rather than directly with capital. Well, all I would like to do here is express a certain scepticism as to whether the ANC in government would be qualitatively more favourable to working class interests than, say, the British Labour Party or the Italian Communist Party in the mid 1970s. I say this partly from observation of the recent evolution of ANC policy, where the tendency has been to play down any intention significantly to undermine capitalist control of the economy. In any case this evolution is no doubt dictated by the logic of the negotiating process, since the terms of any settlement are likely to include formal or informal guarantees that capitalist interests will be respected under a democratic constitution. It is quite unrealistic to expect that organised labour can count on the ANC's support when it bargains with capital.

A second 'peculiarity' of South Africa often thought relevant to the fate of a social contract here is the existence of mass unemployment and poverty on a far greater scale than in developed countries and the consequent divisions created within the black working class or indeed between those in employment and the rest of the oppressed population. Sometimes this is held to be a factor favourable to a social contract. The pressure of the impoverished masses would, so the argument goes, prevent the organised working class from drawing too close to capital. More frequently, however, the potential conflicts of interests between skilled and unskilled, employed and unemployed are treated as a factor which might make a social contract unfeasible and/or undesirable in South Africa. Thus von Holdt writes:

> There is a danger ... that if the unions lead a programme of introducing new technology and management techniques, they could increasingly reflect the interests and aspirations of the most skilled articulate workers, and neglect the interests of semi- and unskilled workers.
>
> Such a development could lay the basis for an organised labour aristocracy. This could lead to a more collaborative relationship between unions and management, assisting to revitalise capitalism rather than transform it. The unpaid and less skilled workers would be pushed to the margins of society.[26]

Warnings of a danger of a labour aristocracy are indeed quite fashionable on the South African left. I must say that I find such talk something of a red herring. It is one thing to say that divisions exist among the oppressed and indeed within the working class which can be exploited by reaction: the experience of the past year proves this beyond doubt. It is quite another to argue that beneath these divisions lies the emergence of distinct group of workers whose wage levels and position within the division of labour give them interests which are antagonistic to the mass of lower-paid workers and unemployed and directs them towards an alliance with capital. The concept of the labour aristocracy was never one of Lenin's better contributions to Marxism. It was precisely the high paid, well organised metal workers who were the best candidates for the lable that provided the vanguard of the revolutionary wave which shook Europe at the end of the First World War, from Petrograd to Turin, Berlin and Glasgow.[27] Matters have been further obscured in recent years by attempts to establish that capitalism is currently entering a 'post-Fordist' phase in which a skilled 'core' of the working class is set at odds with a low-paid 'periphery', a theory with scant empirical support.[28]

Belief in an emergent South African labour aristocracy is sometimes reinforced by the idea that social contracts tend to favour the more skilled and better-paid workers. This was certainly not the British experience. Skilled workers—for example, toolmakers in the British Leyland (now Rover) car plants—were the first to strike against the 1974-9 Labour government's pay policy because of its effect in squeezing wage differentials. The 'winter of discontent' in 1978-9 which finally destroyed the Social Contract involved strikes by low paid workers, notably in the National Health Service and the municipalities, but also by much better paid workers such as lorry drivers. But, experience elsewhere aside, what reason is there to believe that a social contract in South Africa will benefit the more highly skilled workers? Nattrass speaks for the consensus when she says that a social contract would require state intervention 'to encourage, cajole and ultimately force South African business into becoming more innovative and competitive'.[29] But what does improved competitiveness entail? Speed ups, possibly reduced wages, probably closures of inefficient plants.

In other words, achieving higher productivity would impose a heavy burden on the workforce—and especially on the highly paid, well organised and more skilled workers who tend to predominate in the unions. Far from benefitting from that social contract, the so called 'labour aristocracy' is likely to be its main target.

This is not to deny that differentiation within the workers' movement is a factor in the movement towards a pact with capital in South Africa. As we have seen, the West European experience of the 1970s involved a growing gulf between union leaders and shop floor. The same kind of process is likely to occur here— namely, a growing antagonism between the rank and file of the unions on the one hand and a bureaucracy of full time officials on the other. The latter's identity as a distinct social layer derives not from their association with any group of workers, as is implied by the concept of a labour aristocracy, but from their social role as mediators between labour and capital.[30] Since a social contract would place a greater emphasis on the pursuit of class compromise it would accelerate the tendency towards a differentiation of a trade union bureaucracy from the general mass of organised workers.

There is in any case a fair amount of evidence that this process is already well under way. One of the interesting things about the Mercedes dispute was that it united full time officials and shop stewards against the bulk of the workforce who opposed a form of bargaining which they believed removed power from the shop floor. A noteworthy feature of the recent pay settlement in the mines was that it made provision for the negotiation of full time stewards. The emergence of a 'shop floor bureaucracy' of full time stewards was a crucial factor in weakening rank and file organisation in the car plants and other militant sectors under the British Social Contract of the late 1970s.[31]

These arguments, if correct, show that social contracts necessarily have damaging consequences for the working class movement. Geoff Schreiner is therefore mistaken when he claims that 'there are good social contracts and bad ones, ones that work and ones that don't, ones that advance the interests of the ruling class and ones that assist in building workers' power and organisation.'[32] Social contracts require the centralisation of power at the top of the trade union movement, in order to facilitate the process of bargaining with capital and the state. And, in return for whatever concessions the ruling class is temporarily prepared to make, restrictions are placed on workers' militancy at the base. Therefore they undermine 'workers' power and organisation'.

This then puts in proper perspective the argument of John Saul that a social contract can be a means of 'ever-expanding working class empowerment', with COSATU's participation in the National Manpower Commission (NMC) serving as a 'front for institutionalising a situation of "dual power" '.[33] Long term collaboration with capital and the state can only weaken the organised working class, not 'empower' it. Moreover, is Saul really saying that by attending meetings of a reformed NMC the workers' movement can somehow colonise a state apparatus whose capacity for reactionary violence has been so dramatically demonstrated in the townships of the Rand?

Underlying Saul's argument is the traditional strategy of Western social democracy: a gradual transition to socialism achieved by first winning control of the existing state. Before buying this project South African socialists should carefully examine the wreckage it has left behind in the developed capitalist countries—the retreat of the parties of the Second International from even Keynesian policies of state intervention to what the **Financial Times** aptly called 'Thatcherism with a human face'. As I suggested earlier, the left in South Africa should seek to learn from the experience of the international working class movement, rather that repeat the latter's mistakes. Far from, as its apologists claim, helping to create the conditions for socialism, a social contract will undermine the most important condition of socialism that already exists in South Africa, namely the organised working class.

Defenders of a social contract may seek to evade my arguments by asking what the alternative is. Before I respond it is worth noting the effrontery of this ploy. The South African left is being asked to buy a strategy which has not simply failed elsewhere, but which has had disastrous consequences—for example, softening up the British workers' movement for the onslaught of Thatcherism. In the hope the unions can somehow drag big business into a repetition of the South Korean 'miracle', apparently forgetting that even if this objective were, most improbably, attained, it would require adopting a 'regime of accumulation' against which the Korean masses have for the past four years been rebelling. The ET Group and their ilk offer a policy which they claim will be both profitable and virtuous, which combines capitalist success and higher levels of welfare. It is incumbent on them to show—as they have singularly failed to do up to now—how on earth they expect to achieve these goals.

What then is the alternative? To reply in detail would take up too much space. Here I can make three points. First, there is much to be said for the tradition of 'militant abstentionism' which von Holdt suggests the South African workers' movement should now abandon.[34] I take 'militant abstentionism' to mean combining the development of strong workplace organisation with a refusal to take any responsibility for the management of South African capitalism. This still remains an entirely rational approach, and not only because of the disastrous consquences likely to follow, as I have argued, any attempt to assist the 'restructuring' of the South African economy. The embyro of an authentically socialist form of society exists in the workplace- and delegate-based democracy that has evolved in the unions. It is through the preservation, strengthening and expansion of these forms that workers can develop their ability to take control of society and run it along radically different lines from those involved in any conceivable variety of capitalism.

Secondly, experience has confirmed beyond doubt that an isolated revolutionary state cannot survive indefinitely. Many socialists, after the East European revolutions and the debacles in Mozambique and Nicaragua, take this as a counsel of despair. But this is a most short sighted conclusion. The past generation has seen the enormous expansion of the world working class—beyond the western capitalist bloc, in the Stalinist countries and in the Newly Industrialising Countries. The result has been, since the beginning of the 1980s, the explosive growth of new workers' movements—Solidarity in Poland, the CUT and Workers Party in Brazil, the South Korean unions, and, of course, COSATU and NACTU in South Africa. The two great miners' strikes in the USSR—of July/August 1989 and March/April 1991—marked the return of the Soviet working class to the historical stage for the first time since October 1917. These developments indicate that an internationalist strategy—a strategy which sees victory in any one country as merely a staging post in a global revolutionary process—can count on far greater forces than when the Bolsheviks first put this strategy to the test in 1917.

Finally, the weakness of the left in South Africa as elsewhere does not lie in objective circumstances, but in what Trotsky called the 'subjective factor'. We are suffering from a crisis of ideas, of will, of imagination. Socialists find themselves unable to conceive of an alternative to capitalism so they settle for tinkering around with capitalism, for market socialism or an improved 'regime of accumulation'. This reflects the grip on their minds of the two dominant socialist traditions—Stalinism and social democracy. The influence of Stalinism for the past two generations has made it almost unavoidable to identify the USSR and its like with socialism, though perhaps of a 'deformed' or 'degenerate' kind. No wonder, then, that the crash of 1989 left so many despairing and confused.

One way out is to abandon Stalinism for social democracy—apparently the path currently followed by the SACP leadership. But, aside from the inherent difficulty of negotiating such a transition (witness the plight of the European Communist Parties), it involves the end of any serious attempt to replace capitalism. Are we really ready to settle for that—especially in a country like South Africa where capitalism has so manifestly failed the bulk of the population? Far better to return to the classical Marxist tradition and its vision of 'socialism from below'. It is there that is to be found the resolution of the ideological crisis gripping the left, not just in South Africa but across the world.[35]

Notes

Abbreviations

FT: Financial Times
SALB: South African Labour Bulletin
WM: Weekly Mail

Introduction

1. Myself included: see A Callinicos, **South Africa between Reform and Revolution**, London 1988 (hereinafter **SARR**), chapter 5, and 'Can South Africa be Reformed?' **International Socialism**, 2:46 (1990) (hereinafter **CSAR**). The latter, twice revised in proof to take account of de Klerk's speech and Mandela's release, reads like a palimpsest of my changing views as the realisation slowly dawned that the NP were going to make the jump. The only comfort is that I was not alone. Thus, a study by two leading liberal political scientists—H Giliomee and L Schlemmer, **From Apartheid to Nation Building**, Cape Town 1989—completed after de Klerk's accession to the NP leadership envisages a slow transition to an ethnically-based political system incorporating the African majority. Two social democratic analysts writing at much the same time described the 'chances' of 'the end of apartheid' by 1996 as 'rather remote': S Terreblanche and N Nattrass, 'A Periodisation of the Political Economy from 1910', in N Nattrass and E Ardington, eds., **The Political Economy of South Africa**, Cape Town 1990, pp. 18-19. See also my interviews with Colin Bundy and Neville Alexander, chapters 4 and 6 above.
2. P Waldmeir, 'Pretoria Takes the Plunge', Survey on South Africa, **FT**, 11 June 1990.
3. See the admirable summary of apartheid's development, ideology and functioning in Giliomee and Schlemmer, **From Apartheid**, chapters 1-3.
4. The relationship between apartheid and capitalism has generated an enormous historical literature, especially since the emergence of the 'revisionist'—in actuality Marxist—school in the early 1970s. See the references given in **SARR**, chapters 1 and 4.
5. S Gelb, 'South Africa's Economic Crisis: An overview', in id., ed., **South Africa's Economic Crisis**, Cape Town 1991, p. 4. The idea that apartheid is a principle factor in accounting for South Africa's

economic performance has recently been challenged. Terence Moll argues that both South Africa's post-war economic growth and its stagnation in the 1980s were in fact typical of 'middle-income developing countries' and that 'external conditions' are chiefly responsible for its pattern of growth: 'From Booster to Brake? Apartheid and Economic Growth in Comparative Perspective', in Nattrass and Ardington, eds., **Political Economy**, p. 83. But even granted the considerable degree to which South Africa's economy depends on the world market, Moll's argument does not take into account the extent to which South Africa has slipped behind other Newly Industrialised Countries (NICs) such as South Korea, Taiwan and Brazil. Thus David Kaplan notes that, 'the capital goods sector in South Africa was comparable to, and in many cases more advanced than, that prevailing in these countries up until the early 1980s. Since that date, the expansion of the capital goods sectors in the NICs has far exceeded that in South Africa', 'The South African Capital Goods Sector and the Economic Crisis', in Gelb, ed., **Economic Crisis**, p. 176. It is conceivable that these trends—symptomatic of South Africa's failure to become a significant exporter of manufactured goods—have nothing to do with apartheid, but Moll fails even to consider them.

6. M McGrath, 'Economic Growth, Income Distribution, and Social Change', in Nattrass and Ardington, eds., **Political Economy**, pp. 99-100.
7. Giliomee and Schlemmer, **From Apartheid**, p. 132; see generally ibid., chapter 4, and **SARR**, especially chapters 2 and 5.
8. See **CSAR**, pp. 99-109, and the interview with Mark Swilling, chapter 1.
9. Survey on South Africa, **FT**, 12 June 1989.
10. Ibid., 7 May 1991.
11. **Independent**, 19 January 1990. This conclusion is confirmed by the best informed study of Umkhonto: H Barrell, **MK: The ANC's Armed Struggle**, Johannesburg 1990.
12. R Aronson, 'Is Socialism on the Agenda?', **Transformation**, 14. (1991), p. 5.
13. **Star**, 12 September 1991.
14. P. Waldmeir, 'In Search of a Coalition', Survey on South Africa, **FT**, 7 May 1991.
15. **Business Day**, 28 November 1990.
16. 'The Pretoria Minute', **Vukani Basebenzi**, September 1990.
17. Waldmeir, 'In Search'.
18. L Vail, ed., **The Creation of Tribalism in Southern Africa**, London 1989.
19. **Independent**, 18 September 1990.
20. G Ruiters and R Taylor, 'Organise or Die', **Work in Progress**, 70/71, November/December 1990, pp. 20-22.

21. Marx and Engels, **Collected Works**, III, London 1975, p. 175.
22. See for example, on the squatter camps of Cape Town, RW Johnson, 'Where Gangsters Rule', **Independent Magazine**, 10 August 1991.
23. **WM**, 19 July 1991.
24. **Independent**, 11 June 1991.
25. **Independent on Sunday**, 7 July 1991, and **Independent**, 19 July 1991.
26. **WM**, 26 July 1991.
27. Ibid., 2 August 1991.
28. Ibid., 9 August 1991.
29. **Independent**, 24 April 1991
30. R Kasrils and Khuzwayo, 'Mass Struggle is the Key', **Work in Progress**, 72, January/February 1991, p. 10. 'Khuzwayo' is apparently a *nom de plume*.
31. Survey on South Africa, **FT**, 7 May 1991.
32. J Baskin, **Striking Back**, Johannesburg 1991, p. 427.
33. Kasrils and Khuzwayo, 'Mass Struggle,' pp. 10-11. Compare the editorial in the SACP journal **Umsebenzi, 6:3.**
34. 'The Path to Power', in **African Communist, 118** (1989), p. 102. For a critique of the two-stage strategy see **SARR**, pp. 65-72. See also the interview with Jeremy Cronin in chapter 3.
35. D Hindson, 'Alternative Urbanisation Strategies in South Africa', **Third World Quarterly, 9:2** (1987).
36. 'Path to Power', p. 120.
37. See **SARR**, pp. 73-6.
38. J Slovo, 'Speech at the 65th Anniversary Meeting of the South African Communist Party, London, 30 July 1986', in **An Alliance Forged in Struggle**, London n.d., p. 10.
39. **WM**, 25 January 1990.
40. **Path to Power**, p. 124.
41. Reprinted in ANC Department of Political Education, **The Road to Peace: Resource Material on Negotiations**, Johannesburg 1990.
42. **Star**, 20 July 1989.
43. The preceding five paragraphs summarise a much more detailed analysis in **CSAR**.
44. K von Holdt, 'COSATU Congress', **SALB**, 16:1, July/August 1991, p. 16. Jeremy Baskin's **Striking Back**, though written from a perspective sympathetic to the COSATU leadership, is, despite some omissions and distortions, a valuable and judicious history of the federation's first five years.
45. See, on the prehistory of COSATU, S. Friedman, **Building Tomorrow Today**, Johannesburg 1987.
46. **SARR**, chapter 4.
47. For contrasting accounts of this period see **SARR**, pp. 167-85, and J Baskin, **Striking Back**, chapters 12 and 13.
48. 'Interview: Moses Mayekiso', **SALB** 14:2, June 1989, pp. 41, 44.

49. See J Baskin, **Striking Back**, pp. 432-7.

50. K von Holdt, 'Editorial Notes', **SALB**, 15:3, September 1990, p. 1. See also this entire issue of the **Labour Bulletin**, which is devoted to the SACP and the future of socialism, and S Phillips, 'The South African Communist Party and the South African Working Class', **International Socialism**, 2:51 (1991). Dlamini's and Mafumadi's earlier membership of the SACP is confirmed in Baskin, **Striking Back**, pp. 62, 66.

51. J Slovo, **Has Socialism Failed?** (London, 1990), reprinted in **SALB**, 14:6, February 1990. The pamphlet attracted some stringent criticism from a Trotskyist perspective: see those by ANC leader Pallo Jordan, 'Crisis of Conscience in the SACP', and by Adam Habib and Mercia Andrews of the Workers Organisation for Socialist Action, 'Disinheriting the Heritage of Stalinism', both in **SALB**, 15:3 September 1990.

52. H Gwala, 'Let Us Look at History in the Round', **African Communist**, 123 (1990).

53. **FT**, 27 February 1990.

54. For the Economic Trends Group, see the issue of **Transformation**, 12 (1990), devoted to its work. The evolution of von Holdt's thinking can be traced in 'Insurrection, Negotiations and "War of Position"', **SALB**, 15:3, September 1990, 'Towards Transforming SA Industry', ibid., 15:6, March 1991, and the paper he gave at the conference on 'Marxism in South Africa—Past, Present and Future', University of the Western Cape, 6-8 September 1991. P Bond, **Commanding Heights and Community Control** (Johannesburg, 1991) is an interesting review of the South African economic debate, though its own solutions are implausible.

55. Baskin, **Striking Back**, pp. 437-40.

56. G Schreiner, 'Fossils from the Past', **SALB**, 16:1, July/August 1991, pp. 35, 37.

57. K von Holdt, 'The Mercedes Sleep-in', **SALB**, 15:4, November 1990, pp. 38-9. This very detailed dossier is all the more admirable because much of the information it provides is inconsistent with von Holdt's evident hostility to the occupation.

58. See A Callinicos, 'The Fire This Time', **International Socialism**, 104, (1978).

59. Baskin, **Striking Back**, pp. 460-1.

60. J Theron, 'Workers Control and Democracy: the Case of FAWU', **SALB**, 15:3 September 1990, pp. 62-3. See, in addition to Theron's lengthy article, D Cooper, 'Trouble in FAWU's Cape Town Branch', and A Roberts, 'Placing the "Campaign for Democracy" in Perspective', **SALB**, 15:2, August 1990, and the correspondence in ibid., 15:4, November 1990.

61. J Saul, 'South Africa: Between "Barbarism" and Structural Reform', **New Left Review**, 188 (1991), p. 6.

62. A Erwin, 'Comments on the Harare Recommendations', **Transformation**, 12 (1990), p. 20.

63. See R Roux, 'National Strike Wave for Wages', **SALB**, 15:2, August 1990, and 'Economic Notes', ibid., 15:8, June 1991.

64. C Cooper, 'Agreement in the Metal Industry', **SALB**, 15:4, November 1990, p. 46.

65. The SACP's disarray in the face of the Moscow coup—Harry Gwala and the Natal Midlands branch backed the conservative Committee for the State of Emergency while an unusually subdued Joe Slovo allowed himself to be bested by Foreign Minister Pik Botha on the South African Broadcasting Corporation's popular TV discussion programme **Agenda**—were signs that the initial burst of growth after the party's unbanning in February 1990 has concealed deeper long-term problems, above all concerning the relationship between the ANC and the SACP. Mandela was reported to have sought to block Slovo's proposed replacement as SACP General Secretary by the popular 'radical' MK Chief of Staff Chris Hani and to be insisting that, after the party's December 1991 conference, SACP leaders holding prominent position inside the ANC should choose which organisation they wished to work in: **Africa Analysis**, 129, 23 August 1991. John Carlin argued that: 'the SACP is no longer a coherent unit but a collection of individuals with a greater or lesser commitment to socialism but an unequivocal identification with "the non-racial democracy" principle of the ANC. Thabo Mbeki, the ANC's able director of international affairs, has allowed his party membership to lapse. Quietly, others will follow; "democratic socialism" will become "social democracy"; the ANC in the manner of erstwhile revolutionary organisations everywhere, will in due course find its place somewhere marginally to the left of the British Labour Party.' **Independent**, 28 August 1991.

Chapter 2.

1. K von Holdt, 'Insurrection, Negotiation and "War of Position"', **SALB**, 15:3, September 1990.

2. K von Holdt, 'The Mercedes Sleep-in', ibid., 15:4, November 1990. See also the introduction.

3. See C Harman, **Gramsci versus Reformism**, London 1983.

4. E Patel, 'The Case for Centralised Bargaining', **SALB** op cit.

5. *'Lekker'* is an almost untranslatable Afrikaans word meaning nice, good or wonderful.

Chapter 3.

1. EJ Hobsbawm, 'Goodbye to All That', **Marxism Today,** October 1990.
2. **South African Communists Speak,** London 1981, pp. 93-4. The introduction of the new policy was part of the Stalinisation of the CPSA, which led to the expulsion of the historic leaders of the party, notably Sidney Bunting.
3. J Cronin, 'Rediscovering our Socialist History', **SALB,** 15:3, September 1990, p. 100.
4. **Umsebenzi, 6:3.**

Chapter 4.

1. **The Ancien Regime and the French Revolution** (London 1966), p. 196.
2. C Bundy, 'History, Revolution and South Africa', **Transformation,** 4 (1987).
3. J Cronin, 'Building the Legal Mass Party', **SALB,** 15:3, September 1990.
4. The contribution made by IB Tabata and the Unity Movement, a group which emerged from the Trotskyist left at the end of the 1930s, to the rural struggles in the Transkei during the 1940s and 1950s is discussed in C Bundy, 'Land and Liberation: Popular Rural Protest and the National Liberation Movement in South Africa 1920-1960' in S Marks and S Trapido, eds., **The Politics of Race, Class and Nationalism in Twentieth-Century South Africa,** London 1987.

Chapter 5.

1. The 'two hats' debate developed after the SACP's legal launch in July 1990. The fact that a number of leading trade unionists also held prominent positions in the SACP national or regional structures caused some concerns in the unions about the divided loyalties this might create. See, for example, J Copelyn, 'Collective Bargaining', and S Zikalala, 'Overlapping Leadership in Alliance Partners', **SALB,** 15:6, March 1991.

Chapter 6.

1. Harold Wolpe, a leading SACP intellectual, was one of the major
    forces in the explosion of South African Marxist scholarship which
    began in the early 1970s. The kind of formulation Alexander has in
    mind is, 'The relationship between capitalism and white domination
    must be seen as an historically contingent, not a necessary one.
    Moreover, that relationship will be both functional and
    contradictory—functional for the reproduction of certain relations
    and contradictory for others ... the formation of structures and
    relations is always the outcome of struggles between contending
    groups of classes and ... this outcome is Janus-faced, being always
    simultaneously functional and contradictory. Which pole of the
    relationship will be dominant depends on the historically specific
    conditions of the social formation': H Wolpe, **Race, Class and the
    Apartheid State**, London 1988, p. 8.
2. A Callinicos, **South Africa between Reform and Revolution**,
    (London 1988), pp. 158-67.
3. The report of the Fagan commission, published in February 1948,
    proposed the acceptance by the South African state of African
    urbanisation and a relaxation of the pass laws. Supported by the
    United Party government of JC Smuts, it was rejected by the
    opposition National Party, who proceeded, after winning the
    general election of May 1948, to implement a programme of
    intensified segregation. See, for example, D Hindson, **Pass
    Controls and the Urban African Proletariat in South Africa** ,
    Johannesburg 1987, chapter 4.
4. J Saul and S Gelb, **The Crisis in South Africa**, rev. edn., London
    1986, pp. 67-76.
5. The distinction between West and Central European approaches to
    the national question was made by Alexander in his paper, 'The
    National Question in South Africa/Azania', given at the Conference
    on 'Marxism in South Africa—Past, Present and Future', University
    of the Western Cape, 6-8 September 1991. Otto Bauer, Karl Renner
    and other leaders of the Austrian Social Democratic Party sought
    before 1918 to preserve the unity of the Austro-Hungarian empire
    by proposing that its constituent nationalities be given political and
    cultural autonomy, a position which was strongly criticised by
    Lenin: see M Löwy, 'Marxists and the National Question', **New Left
    Review**, 96 (1976).
6. Alexander's multi-lingual solution involves, in particular,
    standardising the different African languages into two, bringing
    together the main language groupings, Nguni and Sotho-Tswana:
    see **The Language Question in South Africa**, Johannesburg
    1989.

7. See T Lodge, **Black Politics in South Africa since 1945**, London 1983, chapters 9 and 10.
8. In August 1991 the SAP opened fire on a demonstration mounted by the Afrikaner Weerstandsbewiging which was trying to prevent de Klerk from addressing a rally in Ventersdorp, where the AWB had its headquarters. Several weeks later, in another sign of the government's willingness to defy the far right, it successfully sat out a hunger strike by three members of another white extremist grouping, the Orde Boerevolk, who had been charged with a number of violent crimes, despite appeals from Mandela for the government to retreat. After the press published photographs of the supposedly dying hunger strikers looking remarkably well, they ended their fast on 9 September, in a humiliating climb-down.
9. 5 Recce, a unit of the SADF Special Forces composed of black mercenaries, is alleged to have taken part in the violence which erupted on the Rand in July 1990; see Introduction.
10. The main Trotskyist gouping persuing an entryist perspective in South Africa is the Marxist Workers Tendency, sister organisation of the British Militant: see my **South Africa between Reform and Revolution**, pp. 104-9.
11. The Workers Party in Brazil, which developed from the militant union movement that sprang into life at the beginning of the 1980s, though social democratic in leadership and programme, contains within its ranks a number of Trotskyist tendencies.
12. The National Forum Committee, formed in 1983, brought together the black consciousness Azania People's Organisation with a number of largely like-minded organisations; CAL and its affiliates were also involved and Alexander is widely credited with authorship of the Azania Manifesto which became the platform of the National Forum.

Afterword.

This afterword was first given as a paper at the Conference on 'Marxism in South Africa—Past, Present and Future', University of the Western Cape, 6-8 September 1991. In a reply to my paper, Mike Morris, a member of the Economic Trends Research Group accused me of amalgamating different positions and thus, for example, running together Nicoli Nattrass's views with the very different ones of the ET Group. My aim was, however, to identify and criticise an emerging consensus on the South African left, even though that consensus is expressed in different ways. One of the most explicit defences of a social contract was indeed given by Geoff Schreiner, COSATU's chief negotiator in its talks with SACCOLA and the Department of Manpower (see Introduction), in a paper first delivered to the ET Group, which I only read after completing the original version of this afterword: 'Fossils from the Past', **SALB**, 16:1, July/August 1991.

1. R Aronson, 'Is Socialism on the Agenda? A letter to the South African Left', **Transformation,** 14 (1991).
2. Ibid., p. 9.
3. Ibid.
4. D Hindson, 'Alternative Urbanisation strategies in South Africa', **Third World Quarterly,** 9:2 (1987).
5. See, for example, the case-studies in S Gelb, ed., **South Africa's Economic Crisis,** Cape Town 1991.
6. R Aronson, op cit., p. 10.
7. LD Trotsky, **The Third International after Lenin,** New York 1970.
8. N Harris, **Of Bread and Guns,** Harmondsworth 1983, and **The End of the Third World,** London 1986.
9. **Business Day,** 12 December 1990.
10. Aronson, 'Socialism', p. 11.
11. It is thus misleading to argue, as, for example the Workers Organisation for Socialist Action (WOSA) has, that the East European revolutions have produced a 'change in the world balance of forces [which] has lengthened our perspective. Socialist society will come but it may take much longer than most socialists ever imagined': 'The International Context of Our Struggle', statement by the WOSA chairperson, (Neville Alexander) 31 May 1991. As part of its strategy during the Cold War, the USSR supported certain revolutionary nationalist regimes in the Third World. This was very far from being a policy of promoting socialist revolution—as the conduct of, for example, the Ethiopian *Derg* clearly shows.
12. See the issue of **Transformation,** 12 (1990), devoted to the work of the ET Group.
13. D Kaplan, 'Recommendation on Post Apartheid Economic Policy', ibid., p. 22
14. See, for example, Stephen Gelb's introductory essay in **South Africa's Economic Crisis.**
15. R Brenner and M Glick, 'The Regulation Approach: Theory and History', **New Left Review,** 188 (1991).
16. M Aglietta, **A Theory of Capitalist Regulation,** London 1979.
17. See the interesting discussion of South Korea in AH Amsden, 'Third World Industrialisation', **New Left Review,** 182 (1990).
18. For example P le Roux, 'The Case for a Social-Democratic Compromise', in N Nattrass and E Ardington, eds., **The Political Economy of South Africa,** Cape Town 1990.

19. **Financial Times**, 8 November 1990. See, more generally, C Sparks and S Cockerill, 'Goodbye to the Swedish Model', **IS** 2:51 (1991).
20. N Nattrass, 'The "Social Contract" Needs Some Central Co-ordination', **WM**, 12 July 1991.
21. K von Holdt, 'Towards Transforming SA Industry', **SALB**, 15:6 (1990), pp 22, 25.
22. See **SALB** 15:4 (1990), which was largely devoted to the Mercedes dispute.
23. **WM**, 2 August 1991.
24. Ibid., 12 July 1991.
25. The best overview of the West European upturn and its aftermath is C Harman, **The Fire Last Time**, London 1988.
26. Von Holdt, 'Towards Transforming', pp. 24-5.
27. See the critique of Lenin's theory of labour aristocracy in T Cliff, 'The Economic Roots of Reformism' in id., **Neither Washington Nor Moscow**, London 1982; D Gluckstein, **The Western Soviets**, London 1985.
28. See A Callinicos and C Harman, **The Changing Working Class**, London 1987, and A Callinicos **Against Postmodernism**, Cambridge 1989, chapter 5.
29. **WM**, 12 July 1991.
30. See T Cliff and D Gluckstein, **Marxism and the Trade Unions**, London 1986, part one.
31. See T Cliff, 'The Balance of Class Forces in Britain Today', **IS** 2:6 (1979); C Harman, '1984 and the Shape of Things to Come', **IS** 2:29.
32. Schreiner, 'Fossils', p. 35.
33. J Saul, 'South Africa: Between "Barbarism" and Structural Reform', **New Left Review**, 188 (1991), p. 38.
34. K von Holdt, 'Towards Transforming', p. 24.
35. I develop the case for classical Marxism at much greater length in **The Revenge of History**, Cambridge 1991.

Index

Adamishin, A: 92
African National Congress: 7,
11, 18, 19-20, 26, 39, 85, 134
—and Congress Alliance,
'Revolutionary Alliance':
32-3, 40
—and COSATU: 13, 16
—economic policy: 49, 57,
69, 72
—and Inkatha violence:
21-2, 24
—signs accord with
government and Inkatha: 38-9
—and Mercedes dispute: 35
—and SACP: 19, 85
—strategy in 1980s: 29-31, 93,
123
—strategy in 1990s: 43-8, 86-7,
106, 135, 145, 148
—concerns about strategy: 16,
26-7, 88-9, 95-6, 122, 124-5,
126-8, 129
—suspends armed struggle: 20
—splits between moderates
and hardliners: 28
Afrikaner
Weerstandsbewiging: 14, 24,
162n
Aglietta, M: 143
Alexander, N: 7, 114-36, 162n
Alexandra: 25
Alexandra Action
Committee: 105

Andrews, M: 158n
Anglo-American Corporation:
29, 65
Angola: 30, 42, 92
Apartheid (see also: Economy):
—history: 12-14
—'grand apartheid': 21
—and capitalism: 115-120,
155-6n, 161n
Aronson, R: 16-17, 138-141
Australia: 143, 148
Austro-Marxism: 120-1, 161n
Azania Manifesto: 162n
Azania People's
Organisation: 162n

Bantu languages: 121, 122
Bantustans: 17
Baskin, J: 27, 36, 157n
Basson, N: 25
Bauer, O: 120, 161n
Beinart, W: 91
Benn, A: 56
Bethlehem, R: 19
Black Consciousness: 31, 52,
81, 119
Botha, Major L: 24
Botha, PW: 13, 16, 30, 41, 46,
91, 94, 117
Botha, RF (Pik): 25, 126, 159n
Brazil: 74
—CUT: 153
—Workers Party: 135, 153, 162n

Brenner, R: 142
Britain
—Labour government: 35-6, 147
—Labour Party: 59, 109, 148
—miners' strike: 36
—social contract: 35-6, 37, 63, 65, 107-8, 147- 52
British Leyland (Rover): 36, 150
British Trade Union Congress: 147
Broederbond: 125-6
Bundy, C: 7, 91-104, 160n
Bush, G: 141
Buthelezi, M (*see also: Inkatha Freedom Party*): 11, 24, 38-9
—and Mandela: 24

Cape Action League: 114, 162n
Carlin, J: 21, 26
Carrillo, S: 89
Chamber of Mines: 145
Chile: 73, 126
China: 75, 84
Civic associations (civics): 41, 48, 52-3, 111, 130, 145
Civil Cooperation Bureau: 25
'Clientelism': 101
Coetzee, Capt. D: 25
'Colonialism of a Special Type': 28
Commercial and Catering Workers Union of South Africa: 32
Communist International: 78, 80, 82, 84
Congress for a Democratic Future: 30
Congress of South African Trade Unions: 13, 72, 134, 153
—and alliance with ANC: 30-2, 122, 128, 148
—arguments between workerists and populists: 32
—and bureaucracy: 36-7
—campaign against LRAA: 34

—and democracy: 40, 63
—4th Congress: 31
—and Freedom Charter:32
—participates in National Manpower Commission: 64-65, 151
—policy: 105, 107, 142
—and 'Revolutionary Alliance': 32-3
—and SACP: 100, 112-3
—and violence: 23, 27
Conservative Party (Konserwatiwe Party): 14, 16, 18, 24, 123
'Consociation': 42, 120
Constituent assembly: 125, 130
'Constitutional Guidelines': 29
Council for Scientific and Industrial Research: 46
Crocker, C: 92
Cronin, J: 7, 33, 76-90, 100, 113
Cuito Cuanavale: 92
Cyprus: 12

Debt: 15
De Klerk, FW: 11, 14-15, 16-17, 18-19, 25-6, 30, 41-3, 87-8, 92, 94-5, 115, 116-7, 123, 124, 127, 128
Democratic Party: 16, 30
Democratic Turnhalle Alliance: 45
Derg: 163n
Development Bank of South Africa: 46
Dlamini, C: 32, 158n
Du Plessis, B (Minister of Finance): 12, 15

East European revolutions: 7, 17, 33, 45, 59, 67, 76, 78, 82, 103, 110, 117, 127, 128-9, 137, 140-1, 152, 163n
East Germany: 17
Economic Trends Research Group: 34, 37, 56, 142, 152, 162-3n
Economy (*See also Apartheid:*

—*and capitalism*): 11, 12-13, 15, 42, 47-8, 93, 124, 138-9, 155-6n
Electricity Supply Commission: 46
Erwin, A: 37
Eurocommunism: 55-6
European Community: 144

'Factory Tribalism': 35-6, 62
Fagan Commission: 116, 161n
Federation of South African Trade Unions: 31, 32, 81
—and violence: 23
Fiat: 147
Fifth Reconnaissance Regiment ('5 Recce'): 25, 127, 162n
Five Freedoms Forum: 30, 43
Food and Allied Workers Union: 36-7
France
—Socialist Party: 56, 57, 140
Freedom Charter: 29, 49-50

Gelb, S: 116
Giliomee, H: 7, 14
Glick, M: 142
Godsell, R: 65, 145
Gomomo, J: 32
Gramsci, A: 56, 60n, 83, 87
Greece: 101
Group Areas Act: 17
'Group Rights': 42
Gwala, H: 33, 99, 159n

Habib, A: 158n
Hani, C: 28, 159n
Harare Declaration: 20, 30, 32
Has Socialism Failed?: 33, 79
Hawke, R: 143
Heath, E: 147
Hirst, P: 50
Hobsbawm, E: 76
Homelands: (*see Bantustans*)
Honecker, E: 17
Hostels
—and unions: 66

—and violence: 22-3, 38
Huntington, S: 94, 125

Influx control: 97-8
Inkatha Freedom Party: 11, 19, 125
—and accord with ANC: 38-9
—and violence: 21-7, 122
'Inkathagate': 24-6
Institute for a Democratic Alternative for South Africa: 30, 43-4
Interim Leadership Group (SACP): 32, 76, 99, 105
International Monetary Fund: 69
International Socialists of South Africa: 8, 40
Iranian Revolution: 29, 70, 82, 129, 131
Iraq: 84
Italy
—Christian Democrats: 45, 147
—Communist Party: 61, 147, 148
—Historic Compromise: 37, 61, 63, 107, 147, 148

Japan: 45, 140
Jordan, P: 158n

Kabwe Conference: 96
Kane Berman, J: 44
Kaplan, D: 7, 142, 156n
Kasrils, R: 26-7, 28
Kautsky, K: 139
Kettledas, L: 64
Khayelitsha: 97-8
Khuzwayo, M: 27, 28
Koevoet: 25
Köpke, C: 35
Krenz, E: 17

Laboria Minute: 34
Labour aristocracy: 149-50
Labour Bulletin: (*see* **South African Labour Bulletin**)

Labour Party (South Africa): 18
Labour Relations Amendment
Act: 23, 31, 34, 64
Land Acts: 17
Language question: 119-20,
121, 122-3, 161n
Latin America: 43, 101
Laurence, P: 17
Lebanon: 120
Lenin, VI: 33, 43, 83, 84, 92,
139, 141, 149
Le Roux, P: 143
Lewis, J: 7
Liberal Democratic Party
(Japan): 45
Lombard, J: 15
Lula (Luís Inácio da Silva): 74
Luxemburg, R: 50

MK (see Umkhonto weSizwe)
Mafumadi, S: 32, 158n
Malan, M: 25
Mandela, N: 15, 26, 30, 35, 40,
123, 159n, 162n
—intervenes to end
strikes: 38
—and Buthelezi: 24
—released: 7, 11
—signs agreement with
Inkatha: 39
Martov, L: 139
Marx, K: 23, 33, 104, 140, 141
Marxism, in South Africa:
31, 115
Marxist Theory Group: 7, 91
Marxist tradition: 59-60, 67-8,
141, 152-3
Marxist Workers Tendency of
the African National Congress:
37, 102, 162n
Mass Democratic
Movement: 14
Mayekiso, M: 7, 32-3, 35, 40,
64, 99n, 105-113
Mbeki, G: 91
Mbeki, T: 159n
Mercedes Benz: 35-6, 56, 57,
60, 61-2, 72, 145, 150-1

Metal and Allied Workers
Union: 105
Migrant labour system
—and violence: 22-3
Mitterrand, F: 57, 140
Moll, T: 156n
Morris, M: 162n
Mozambique: 25, 153
Mugabe, R: 87, 100

Naidoo, J: 31
Namibia: 25, 30, 42, 92
National bargaining: 35, 62-3
National Bargaining Forum: 35
National Council of Trade
Unions: 31, 100, 134, 153
—campaign against LRAA: 34
National Forum Committee:
48n, 114, 135, 162n
National Language Project: 114
National Management System:
14, 41n
National Manpower
Commission: 34, 64, 151
National Party:
—architects of apartheid:
12-13, 21
—constitutional plans: 17-20
—divisions between
'pragmatists', 'strategists' and
'ideologues': 19
—parliamentary caucus:14, 41n
—seeks negotiated
settlement: 11
—strategy: 7, 41-7, 120, 124,
125, 126-8, 135
National question: 120-1, 161n
National Union of
Metalworkers of South Africa:
27, 35, 59, 62, 63, 66, 99, 105,
107, 145, 148
—abandons 1990 strike:
38, 122
—adopts freedom charter: 32
National Union of
Mineworkers: 32, 145
'Native Republic': 78
Nattrass, N: 144, 145-6, 162n

Nicaragua: 75, 153
Nove, A: 140
Nzo, A: 16

'Operation Agree': 25
Orde Boerevolk: 162n
Organisation for African
Unity: 20

Pan Africanist Congress: 11,
31, 51-2, 59, 124, 135
Pass Laws
—abolished: 14
Patel, E: 64
Path to Power: 28-9, 30
Phillipines: 129
Pillay, D: 7, 34, 55-75
Planact: 41
Planning: 67-8, 74-5, 110-111
Population Registration
Act: 17
'Populists': 31-2, 40, 81
Poqo: 124
Portugal: 82, 89, 101
Pretoria Minute: 20

Rand Revolt: 77
Regulation School: 142-3
Relly, G: 29
Renamo: 25
Renner, K: 120, 161n
Reserve Bank: 72
Rhodesia (see also:
Zimbabwe): 25
Rivonia Treason Trial: 15
Robinson, J: 146
Rockman, G: 42
Ruiters, G: 22
Russian Revolution: 74, 75, 77,
102, 133, 139

Sao Paulo: 74
Saul, J: 37, 116, 151
Schlemmer, L: 14, 44
Schreiner, G: 34-5, 151, 163n
Security Branch: 24
'Securocrats': 41
Sharpeville: 124n

Shop stewards
—democracy: 63, 73, 141
—full time: 35, 36, 37, 66,
72, 150
Slovo, J: 29-30, 33, 35, 40, 49,
79, 82, 85, 140
—and Moscow coup: 159n
Smuts, J: 77n
Social contract (see also
Britain: social contract; Italy:
Historic Compromise; Spain:
Moncloa Pact): 34-9, 66-7,
106-8, 137, 144-52
Social democracy: 33-4, 50, 57,
72, 143, 153
'Socialism in One
Country': 139
Solidarnosc: 153
South African Breweries: 38
South African Commercial,
Catering and Allied Workers
Union: 65
South African Committee for
Higher Education: 114.
South African Communist
Party:
—and alliances: 16, 19, 27
29-33, 122
—history: 77-8, 160n
—and Mercedes: 145
—and Moscow coup: 40, 127,
159n
—role in transition from
apartheid: 98-101, 112, 124,
128, 135
—7th Congress: 28
—strategy: 129, 133,
—transformation of: 49-51, 76,
105, 137, 153
—unbanned: 11
—and unions: 59, 65, 71
South African Consultative
Committee on Labour
Affairs: 34
South African Defence Force:
14, 131, 132-3
—involvement in township
violence: 25-6

South African Labour Bulletin: 33, 40, 55, 60, 64, 80
South African Police: 131, 132
—complicity in township violence: 24, 127
South African Railways: 38
South America (*See Latin America*)
South Korea: 74, 143, 152, 153
South West African People's Organisation: 25, 45n
Southern Europe: 43
Soweto (1976 rising): 13, 81, 84-5
Spain: 89, 94, 98, 101, 147
—Communist Party: 147
—Moncloa Pact: 147
—Suarez government: 147
Squatter camps: (see also Khayelitsha)
—and violence 22-3
Stalinism: 33, 50, 59, 67-8, 69, 70, 71, 79-81, 153
State of Emergency: 14, 29, 31, 41, 126,
State power, and insurrection: 51-2, 59, 69, 73-5, 129-33
State Security Council: 14, 41n
Suarez, A: 94, 147
Sweden: 67, 143-4, 146, 148
Swilling, M: 7, 40, 41-54

Tabata, IB: 103, 160n
Tambo, O: 29
Taylor, R: 22
Thatcher, M (and Thatcherism): 16, 57, 67, 108, 143, 147, 151-2
Theron, J: 37
Tocqueville, A de: 91
Trade unions, (*see COSATU, NACTU, Mercedes, Shop stewards, NUM, NUMSA and others*)
Transvaal Provincial Administration: 108
Tricameral Parliament (1983 Constitution): 14, 18, 94

Trotsky, L: 52, 102, 139, 153
Trotskyism; 40, 69, 70, 71, 74, 75, 102, 114
Tshwete, S: 35
'Two hats' debate: 112-3, 160n
'Two stage strategy': 28-9, 31, 83-4, 97, 133

Umkhonto weSizwe (MK): 16, 28, 93, 124
Umsebenzi: 81, 86, 88
United Democratic Front: 30, 48n
United States: 30, 92, 117-8, 140, 143
United Workers Union of South Africa: 25
Unity Movement: 59, 102, 114, 160n
Urban Foundation: 48
USCO Steel: 27
USSR: 30, 79, 80, 92, 93, 129, 153
—Moscow coup: 40, 128, 134, 159n

Van Zyl Slabbert, F: 43, 44n
Ventersdorp: 127, 162n
Verwoerd, H: 21, 41
Viljoen, G: 125
Vlok, A: 26
Von Holdt, K: 7, 32-3, 34, 55-75, 144-5, 148, 149, 152
Vorster, BJ: 41, 117

Waldmeir, P: 19
Webster, E: 7
Western Europe: (see also separate countries) 55, 68, 144, 146-8
—Communist parties: 56
Winter of Discontent: 150
Wolpe, H: 93, 116, 161n
Work in Progress: 55
'Workerists': 31-2, 81, 99
Workers Charter: 105, 109
Workers councils: 70, 72, 75, 82

Workers Organisation for Socialist Action: 8, 40, 59, 102, 114, 125, 134, 135, 158n, 163n
Working class
—labour aristocracy: 149-50
—rise of skilled blacks: 13
—structure of: 65, 117
—and urbanisation: 28-9
—world: 74, 153
World Bank: 69

Yeltsin, BN: 135
Yu Chi Chan Club: 114

Zimbabwe: 46, 87, 90, 100-1, 131
Zimbabwe African National Union-Patriotic Front: 90, 100, 131

Other publications from Bookmarks

Fighting the Rising Stalinist Bureaucracy: Trotsky 1923-27 / *Tony Cliff*

A new and original account of Trotsky's defence of the Russian Revolution which differs from all others in showing both that he had a real alternative to Stalin, and why he failed. 320 pages. £6.95 / $11.95

Year One of the Russian Revolution / *Victor Serge*

The classic account of the trials and triumphs of the first workers' state. The life and death battles between classes and parties over the fate of the revolution come to life through its pages. 460 pages. £12.95 / $22.50

Marxism and the Trade Union Struggle / *Tony Cliff and Donny Gluckstein*

An analysis of the dynamics, strengths and limitations of trade union organisation. This book centres on the British General Strike of 1926, but contains valuable insights for trade unionism everywhere. 320 pages. £6.95 / $11.95

Nicaragua: What Went Wrong? / *Mike Gonzales*

Traces the road taken by the Sandinistas from mass insurrection in 1979 to electoral defeat in 1990, indentifying the central weaknesses in their strategy. 144 pages. £4.50 / $7.95

South Africa between Reform and Revolution / *Alex Callinicos*

This book charts the development of apartheid and the long-brewing crisis of the 1970s and 1980s. Valuable background to today's fast moving events. 242 pages. £4.95 / $8.50

The Revolutionary Ideas of Karl Marx / *Alex Callinicos*
It is over a century since Marx analysed capitalism as a
world system prone to repeated wars, recessions and
upheavals. His ideas have never been more vindicated
than they are today, and yet he is villified and dismissed
the world over. This book sets out to retrieve the real
Marxist tradition. 208 pages. £3.95 / $7.95

The Changing Working Class / *Alex Callinicos and Chris
Harman*
Capitalism continually revolutionises production, and
does the same to the working class. Does this mean
today's white collar workers are really middle class? Has
the traditional manual working class disappeared? Is the
workforce now split between a core and periphery?
112 pages. £3.50 / $6.75

State Capitalism in Russia / *Tony Cliff*
The unsurpassed analysis of the class society built by
Stalin over the ruins of the Russian Revolution.
Indispensible for understanding the world today. With
new introduction covering the Gorbachev years.
377 pages. £5.95 / $9.00

The Fire Last Time / *Chris Harman*
A major study of the upheavals which rocked the world at
the end of the long boom, and their aftermath. Crucial for
understanding how the rulers that trembled in the late
1960s and early 1970s managed to survive the following
decades of recession. 406 pages. £6.95 / $13.50

All available from good bookshops, or by post from Bookmarks
(add 10 percent for postage).
BOOKMARKS
265 Seven Sisters Road, London N4 2DE, England.
PO Box 16085, Chicago, Il. 60616, USA
GPO Box 1473N, Melbourne 3001, Australia